I0434409

Philosophy of Everyday Life

Philosophy of Everyday Life

Eric Knopp

A Thesis

iUniversity Press
San Jose New York Lincoln Shanghai

Philosophy of Everyday Life

All Rights Reserved © 2000 by Eric Knopp

No part of this book may be reproduced or transmitted in any form or by any means, graphic, electronic, or mechanical, including photocopying, recording, taping, or by any information storage retrieval system, without the permission in writing from the publisher.

iUniversity Press
an imprint of iUniverse.com, Inc.

For information address:
iUniverse.com, Inc.
5220 S 16th, Ste. 200
Lincoln, NE 68512
www.iuniverse.com

Submitted to the Division of Humanities
of New College of the University of South Florida,
in partial fulfillment of the requirements for the degree
of Bachelor of Arts
Under the sponsorship of Professor Douglas Berggren.

Sarasota, Florida
May, 2000

ISBN: 0-595-12245-0

Printed in the United States of America

Contents

Abstract

This thesis deals with the role of ethics in daily life. It examines the meta-physical foundations of the ethics of Socrates and Nietzsche, deriving from those metaphysics broadly applicable ethical recommendations. The introduction presents a general overview of the thesis. The first and second chapters of this thesis examine how the incompatible metaphysical assumptions of Socrates and Nietzsche nevertheless do not preclude their developing compatible ethical worldviews. The third chapter analyzes three literary texts and demonstrates how their protagonists represent three reactions to the ethical possibilities provided in the philosophies of Socrates and Nietzsche. The conclusion discusses what ethical choices are viable today.

Professor Douglas Berggren
Thesis Advisor
Division of Humanities

Introduction

This thesis begins with an assessment of Platonic metaphysics. Plato's metaphysics is widely considered to be the most influential way of thinking in the history of Western thought. As Alfred North Whitehead famously observed:all of philosophy is a footnote to Plato. The first chapter of this thesis considers the most fundamental Platonic metaphysical assumptions. These are the bifurcations which together are commonly known as Platonic dualism. They include, though are not limited to, the dichotomies of soul and body; of being and becoming; and of reason and emotion, passion and madness. The Platonic Socrates is commonly considered in every instance of these dichotomies to subsume the latter to the former; at all times connecting the former with what is eternal and divine, and the latter with what is mortal and changing. The best support for this reading is in the *Phaedo*, which features a discussion of the immortality of the soul, and Socrates' often quoted definition of philosophy as preparation for death. Yet this reading does not present an accurate whole picture of the person of Socrates and the philosophy he develops. Dialogues such as the *Symposium*, the *Phaedrus*, and the *Philebus* suggest that a more sympathetic reading of Socrates is justified. Dialogues such as the *Apology*, the *Crito*, and even in its own unusual way, the *Republic* demonstrate congruences between the person of Socrates and his philosophy. But the intricacies and influences of Platonic metaphysics are already among the most well studied aspects of Western philosophy.

This thesis is not meant only to make clear the already well known implications of Plato's metaphysics. It is simply that such an examination is a necessary prerequisite to an examination of Socratic ethics, which is asserted here to be much more comprehensive than traditionally thought. The traditional reading of Socratic ethics is in keeping with the traditional reading of Platonic metaphysics. For the purposes of this thesis, it is unfortunately necessary to make little distinction between Plato and his teacher and literary creation, Socrates. Socratic ethics is commonly considered to derive from the Platonic/Socratic metaphysics; just as this metaphysics gives primacy to the eternal and unchanging, so the ethics prefers a way of life that values approaching the divine over a way that values what is earthly. Metaphysically, the soul is more real than the body. Similarly, the realm of the forms, representing what is eternal, is more real than the world of becoming. And reason, that uniquely human faculty, is more valuable than instinct, emotion, passion, and madness, because it alone allows human imperfection to approach an understanding of divine perfection. Ethically, Socrates is purported to assert that the body should be utilized only as an instrument for the care of the soul. The imperfect world of becoming should be lived in and approached in such a way as to allow for an indication of the perfect world of being its perception calls to mind. And human reason, according to this view, is the means to the attainment of this most desirable sort of life, which is called the practice of philosophy.

Yet to read Socrates in this way, though convenient in setting him in opposition to later figures in the history of Western thought, is to do him a terrible disservice. In fact, a much more defensible reading, and one which is put forth in the first chapter of this thesis, is both more complex and more sympathetic. Through a close reading of specific dialogues, Socratic thought is demonstrated to include everything it is commonly thought to oppose. In the main, Socratic reason is shown not to exclude the irrational but to require it. This is an important redefinition of human reason, and has many implications which are fleshed out throughout what follows. Socratic reason now includes an appreciation for the bodily and the changing as an important part of the good life inherently, and not merely instrumentally for the good of an immortal soul. The way of life that best serves the immortal soul, turns out to serve human life best regardless of the well-being of the soul. So that the metaphysics which first justified the ethics becomes extraneous, and the ethics remains as demonstrating useful imperatives for everyday life irrespective of metaphysical assumptions or beliefs.

This part of the thesis, then, demonstrates a Socratic ethics with new and wider implications. It characterizes Socrates much more compassionately and compellingly than usual in the tradition. And it demonstrates that the lessons of his life and thought are still useful in spite of later developments that attempted to discredit him. The second chapter moves from Socrates to Nietzsche. Socrates and Nietzsche are often thought of as correspondingly oppositional in every way. Nietzsche is widely considered to reverse Platonic metaphysics, and in many places personally attacks Socrates. The purpose of the second chapter is to demonstrate how this oversimplified reading of Nietzsche is not the case, and does a disservice both to Socrates and to Nietzsche himself. It reads Nietzsche as having submitted to the human failing he is most against:resentment. It wrongs Nietzsche, attributing to him the characteristic in himself he most wants to sublimate. It wrongs Socrates, who does not support the worldview Nietzsche asserts to be his.

The second chapter discusses the ways in which Nietzsche does clearly contradict Platonic metaphysics. Most often, he reverses and eliminates the Platonic dichotomy of soul and body. Whereas Socrates gave primacy to the soul, describing it as being imprisoned in a body which could only do it harm, Nietzsche demands reverence for the body itself. Nietzsche argues that giving primacy to the soul devalues the body in favor of something which almost certainly does not exist. He will maintain a concept of soul only as a useful metaphor for talking about the body. Yet this reversal of Plato really only applies to the discussion of the soul in the *Phaedo*, which occurs as Socrates is about to be executed. Certainly no one would fault Socrates for seeking solace in immortality at such a time. Socrates' definitions of the soul in the *Phaedrus* and the *Philebus* take a much more generous view of the interrelation between body and soul. Nietzsche attacks Socrates unfairly, in that the view he attacks is a very small part of Socratic thought which Nietzsche wrongly portrays as Socratic thought in its entirety.

Nietzsche considers Platonic dichotomies only long enough to demonstrate how their reversal is more conducive to a good human life. He urges belief in the human body itself, in becoming over being, and in instinct over reason. Nietzsche associates Socratic reason with persuasion, rhetoric, deceit, and propaganda. He prefers instinct instead. Instinct is that immediate prompting to right conduct which characterizes the honorable person. Unfortunately, Nietzsche's assessment of Socratic reason is as impoverished as his assessment of the Socratic primacy of the soul. That is, it relies on too narrow a definition of Socratic reason. Much of the first chapter is devoted to defending a redefinition of Socratic reason. This new definition is more like Nietzsche's concept of instinct than like his concept of reason. In this way, Nietzsche is shown to be more like Socrates than he cared to admit.

Perhaps Nietzsche's most well-known and most misunderstood theory is that of the eternal recurrence. A discussion of the eternal recurrence is central to the second chapter of this thesis. The reading which is ultimately most defensible by the texts themselves indicates that belief in the eternal recurrence provides for Nietzsche a similar use as belief in the immortality of the soul provides for Socrates. Socrates relies on his proofs of the immortality of the soul to justify his prescriptions for human life. It is on account of the immortal soul that the body should be regarded a certain way, the faculty of reason exercised in a certain way, and the earthly world approached in a certain way. Human life is regarded as dangerous to the soul, and should be lived in such a way as to preserve the soul in spite of many dangers. As argued in the first chapter, what this actually means is much different from what it is traditionally thought to mean. Contrary to devaluing the body and human life, it prescribes a way of living which is the best available whether the soul is immortal or not. In fact, even if there is no soul, as Nietzsche suggests, Socrates would not then recommend a different way of life. Belief in the soul allows for a certain way of life, whether that belief is true or not.

The similarity to the eternal recurrence is startling. The theory of the eternal recurrence requires that the individual approach his life in a certain way:as if it will recur again and again, eternally. Whether or not it actually will, and it almost certainly won't, does not matter to the theory of the eternal recurrence as interpreted in the second chapter. It is merely a way of thinking about life; a challenge to live well despite many dangers. At least according to the reading defended below. The connection of Socrates' defense of the immortal soul with Nietzsche's formulation of the eternal recurrence is an example of how contradictory metaphysical beliefs can nevertheless engender compatible ethical beliefs. This thesis demonstrates how Socrates and Nietzsche are more similar than not, because what is important, their ethical recommendations, endure even after their metaphysics lose significance.

Reassessing the relationship between Socrates and Nietzsche includes rereading the texts to examine how their thoughts converge in ways previously overlooked. It also includes rereading the character of Socrates and the characters of Nietzsche, both himself and his Zarathustra, to see how what is made explicit in Socratic and Nietzschean philosophy is implicit in their characters. To this end Socratic irony is contrasted with Nietzschean mockery; Socrates' resistance to public opinion is contrasted with Zarathustra's uneasy relationship with his disciples; and Socrates' resistance to writing is contrasted with Nietzsche's faith in the importance of his writing as a process of self-overcoming. What this proves is that much like a close examination of their philosophies, a close examination of their characters demonstrates much more congruence than incompatibility, neverminding Nietzsche's protests to the contrary.

The first chapter reviews and revises Socratic metaphysics and ethics. The second chapter rereads Nietzsche and Nietzschean critiques of Socrates and Plato in view of the arguments of the first chapter. The third chapter considers three short Twentieth century novels, reading them as examples of the existential possibilities provided to individuals by the philosophies of everyday life presented in the first two chapters. Joseph K. of Franz Kafka's *The Trial* represents the difficulty of living well in the absence of Platonic ideals against which to measure oneself. He is never able to get anywhere with his life because he does not realize that without anything external or above, he himself must create his own values and meaning. Consequently, he lives poorly and dies confused. But this is due to a personal failing of Joseph K., not to a failing of Platonic ethics. Platonic ethics endures despite the fact the Platonic metaphysics is no longer a real option for human belief. Socrates himself maintained in circumstance no less absurd than those of Joseph K.

Albert Camus' Meursault, from *The Stranger*, represents the danger of collapsing into nihilism in the absence of Platonic certainty. Unlike K., who is unable to take any effective action in the course of his life, Meursault has not desire to take action. Unlike K., who is unable to explain himself no matter how hard he tries, Meursault has no desire to explain himself. Unlike K., who wants very badly to resolve his situation, Meursault does not care what his situation is. Meursualt's nihilism indicates the danger of abandoning a Platonic way of setting up the world without the preservation of a Socratic way of living in the world.

Aleksandr Solzhenitsyn's Ivan Denisovich Shukhov, from *One Day in the Life of Ivan Denisovich* is a much different character from both Joseph K. and Meursault. Unlike K.'s impotence or Meursault's indifference, Shukhov demonstrates the potential of Nietzschean joyful creativity. Shukhov is constrained by circumstances at least as confining and discouraging as the other two characters. K. is involved in an absurd trial, at the conclusion of which he will be executed; Meursault, at least in the second part of the book, is imprisoned and awaiting execution; and Shukhov is imprisoned in a forced labor camp. Though his death sentence is not as impending, perhaps, as those of the other two, nevertheless Shukhov has little hope for the future. Though his imprisonment is only meant to last ten years, he has no way of knowing if he will be released in a timely fashion, though that seems unlikely, or exiled, or given another ten years. And like Joseph K. and Meursault, how Shukhov arrived in his present situation is absurd and completely out of his control.

There is no disputing the gravity of Shukhov's situation. Yet that gravity does not weigh upon Shukhov like their similar circumstances weigh upon K. and Meursault. Like Nietzsche, Shukhov resists the spirit of gravity. Shukhov strives to create a life for himself by comporting himself within his limitations in the most life-affirming way possible. That this is so is evidenced in many different ways in the text, including the way he relates himself to his present moment despite the absurdity of his past and the dimness of his future; the way he relates himself to others; and the way he functions in the harshness of his environment. So that the third chapter as a whole demonstrates three among an infinite range of possibilities for a philosophy of everyday life, using by way of example three different literary figures.

The purpose of this thesis, then, is to defend a rereading of Socratic ethics; suggest a reassessment of Nietzsche's reaction to Socrates; and demonstrate some possibilities for human life in accordance with Socratic and Nietzschean thought through the examples of three literary characters. The conclusion of this thesis examines whether Nietzsche has successfully responded to Socrates, and whether any of the three fictional characters offers a real example for a philosophic life. The conclusion asks, what ethics is now required for our contemporary time?

Chapter One

Reason and Passion in the Life and Thoughts of Socrates

> *Do you think that there is a kind of good which we should be glad to have for its own sake alone, not because we desire what comes from it? Like joy, and those pleasures which are harmless, and afterwards nothing happens because of them except that you keep on being happy.* [1]

Though the epigram beginning this chapter is from Plato's *Republic*, its significance for the following reading of the Socratic way of life extends far beyond that one dialogue. In this passage Glaucon asks Socrates a question concerning the good which points up both Socrates' unique way of life and the import of Socratic philosophy as it is interpreted here. The good is solidly situated within the eternal and unchanging order of things. Yet it is accompanied by pleasure, which is widely considered oppositely situated among the temporal and imperfect. Here Glaucon is asking Socrates if the good is like pleasure, in that it is worth having simply and for its own sake. Glaucon's assumption is that pleasure, like the good, is something which can be possessed. His question, then, is if there is a good which is worth having in the same way as pleasure is worth having.

It is a good question, but his error is in assuming that pleasure is something tangible. In fact, pleasure is something additional and always accompanying something else. Pleasure can arise along with the satisfaction of

---

[1] Glaucon to Socrates, *Republic*, 357b4–357b8 (Rouse, trans.).

3

bodily needs, as discussed in the *Phaedo*, or along with the search for knowledge, as in the *Phaedrus* and the *Philebus*. Glaucon attempts to connect the good with pleasure, but in the wrong way. Socrates is commonly thought to oppose reason, the primary faculty required for the good life, to pleasure. But in fact they are connected; Glaucon only connects them in the wrong way. Despite how he is often interpreted, Socrates does connect reason and pleasure. Philosophic reason strives toward the good, and pleasure is that sensation which accompanies the striving. The love which is love of wisdom is the pleasure accompanying the search for knowledge. Glaucon does not get this right, but his question is a good place from which to begin developing an understanding of the wide import of the Socratic lifestyle. This important aspect of Socratic thought is one way in which the common misreading of Socrates is challenged here.

In what follows, the Socratic metaphysics which is both so influential and so out of favor is examined from a new perspective:its importance as a source for the Socratic practical ethic. Platonic metaphysics as it is known through the character of Socrates is reread and reinterpreted. The ethic shown to derive from that metaphysics is exemplified by the life of Socrates himself. The Socratic ethic is shown to yield three practical ethical imperatives for the good life. Reading closely dialogues such as the *Symposium*, the *Pheadrus* and *Philebus*, and even the seemingly contradictory *Phaedo* and *Republic*, the significance of this reinterpretation of Socratic thought is demonstrated. Later chapters demonstrate how the Socratic ethic gibes surprisingly with Nietzschean philosophy, and how both of these ethical systems are discernable in otherwise disparate literary characters.

However, this discussion begins with the character of Socrates. The person of Socrates, as he exists through Plato, discovers truths through conversation while living in a manner which is for the most part convincingly consonant with these truths. The subtending assumption of eternal and unchanging truths informing Socrates' thinking and being makes this situation even more interesting, from a literary and a philosophic perspective. But it is in the main the philosophic perspective with which this excursion is concerned. Reading Plato's Socrates requires from the reader constant vigilance, insofar as a fascinating strain of thought is often progressing clandestinely, concealed behind several textual layers of meaning, allusion, and even narrative plot.

This chapter will examine Socrates' metaphysical assumptions and demonstrate how he derives from these ethical imperatives for living the best possible life. Throughout it will be seenhow the metaphysical and ethical are intertwined, and the significance of this will be seen in the following chapter, where it is demonstrated how contrary metaphysical assumptions can yield remarkably similar ethical imperatives. Socrates' metaphysics is illustrated by three binary oppositions recurring continually throughout the Platonic dialogues. These are:the primacy of the immortal soul over the mortal body; the primacy of eternal and unchanging perfect being over imperfect becoming; and the primacy of the human faculty of reason over divinely inspired and irrational madness. Clearly, these three oppositions are connected with one another in the Socratic metaphysics. What may not be so clear is how and why this metaphysics yields for Socrates certain very real imperatives an individual will follow if concerned for living the best possible life.

These three metaphysical oppositions yield three ethical imperatives, which are called here the Socraticimperatives. In the next chapter, these will be contrasted with Nietzsche's imperatives as discerned in his philosophic texts in order to indicate how contradictory metaphysics can produce harmonious ethics. All three Socratic imperatives are connected with all three metaphysical assumptions. They are:virtuous right-living, in which the practice of virtues such as self-control prepare the soul for its ascension to the realm of the forms after death; exercise of the faculty of reason, in which Socrates redefines reason and asserts its role in the good human life; and allowing becoming to approach being, in which the individual lives in such a way as to create possibilities for the inherent imperfection of his life to approach divine perfection This is the practice of philosophy, and it benefits both earthly existence and the soul itself after it is no longer imprisoned in a body. Clearly all three of these imperatives are so closely related as to be almost inseparable from one another. Yet an analysis of the Platonic dialogues will demonstrate the connections among the character of Socrates, his metaphysics, and his ethics.

A first glance at the character of Socrates straightaway leads the reader to the belief that he is before anything else a logically-thinking man. Plato demonstrates this in countless places, but especially in a certain passage from the *Symposium*, where Alcibiades draws explicit attention to Socrates' manner of discussion. This passage, quoted below, is one of many examples of the droll subtlety of Socrates' thought. In fact, even in the *Apology* Socrates himself demonstrates, as part of his unsuccessful defense, the public reaction to,and its misinterpretation and perpetual misunderstanding of, his apparently inscrutable lifestyle. But Socrates has long understood the danger of public opinion, and never, even up until his death, as one learns from both the *Crito* and the *Phaedo*, accords it any value.[2] With respect to these ideas, one reading of Socrates is this. In the *Symposium* Alcibiades likens Socrates to a silenus, a type of statue which is ugly on the outside, but which, when broken open, contains within something beautiful and valuable. Alcibiades explains,

> For were one willing to hear Socrates' speeches, they would at first look altogether laughable. The words and phrases that they wrap around themselves on the outside are like that, the very hide of a hybristic satyr. For he talks of pack-asses, blacksmiths, shoemakers, and tanners, and it looks as if he is always saying the same things through the same things; and hence every inexperienced

---

[2] Socrates asks Crito, "And, therefore, in questions of justice and injustice, and of the base and the honorable, and of good and evil, which we are now examining, ought we to follow the opinion of the many and fear that, or the opinion of the one man who understands these matters (if we can find him), and feel more shame and fear before him than before all other men" *Crito*, 47c8-47d3 (Church, trans.)?

and foolish human being would laugh at his speeches. But if one sees them opened up and gets oneself inside them, one will find, first, that they alone of speeches have sense inside; and, second, that they are most divine.... [3]

This is Socrates' unique style:Socrates talks around the issue at hand in such as way as ineluctably to draw the interlocutor's attention to a difficult idea without his even noticing it until it is too late. Socrates' dialectic is a kind of spoken-word legerdemain. Alcibiades believes that although Socrates may have tricked the others, Alcibiades has caught onto this truth.

Interestingly enough, Alcibiades' accusation is resonant with those of Anytus, Meletus, and others as presented in the *Apology*. Here is the well-known accusation that Socrates corrupts the young by teaching them how the lesser is in fact the greater cause. In this dialogue more than any other, Socrates defines and defends his position, and is so successful that he appears even more victorious for having been found guilty than if he had been acquitted, as it seems to the reader he should have been, had justice been served. His superior position in this dialogue is continued in the related dialogues, *Phaedo* and *Crito*. Rather than summarize the arguments Socrates employs in his defense, it is instructive to see how his style of argument is consistent with his way of life, as far as the reader learns from the other dialogues, up until this point. Socrates believes in what he calls right-living. That is, in putting nothing before virtue, not even when there is a danger of death:"A man who is good for anything ought not to calculate the chance for living or dying; he ought only to consider whether in doing anything he is doing right or wrong."[4]This defense of the virtuous life contained within the idea of right-living is the first of the Socratic imperatives that will be demonstrated here.

---

[3] *Symposium*, 221e1–222a4 (Bernadete, trans.).
[4] *Apology*, 28b5-28b8 (Jowett, trans.).

This imperative is reflected in the manner in which Socrates conducts himself throughout the course of his trial. He is systematic:he recapitulates his accusers' arguments (as always, the reader intuits, in language better than any available to the accusers themselves), assesses and dismisses them, and presents his own position. Found guilty, Socrates shows how he will nevertheless be better off than his accusers, in large part because, "Nothing will injure me, not Meletus nor yet Anytus—they cannot, for a bad manis not permitted to injure a better than himself."[5] Socrates possesses the strength of his convictions, so that one feels he truly lives as he believes. The dialogues mentioned so far have much to recommend them, most notably the way the character of Socrates comes through in the action of the narrative and the conversations, and the way important Platonic beliefs are asserted and defended. But their narrow purpose here is simply to illustrate the fact that Socrates is logical and compelling in both speech and action.

The conjunction of logic and compulsion characterizes Socrates' philosophic style from the earliest dialogues until the last of those in which he appears. He deploys reason so as to be able accurately to examine a situation or belief, yet his initial impetus is at the prompting of Apollo (for example, his *Apology*), or his inner voice which never misguides him (*Apology*, *Phaedrus*), or a muse or spirit (*Phaedrus*). Socrates' fundamental belief is that the individual ought to care more for the soul than the body,and that philosophy is the finest way to go about this.[6] This idea recurs continually and is arguably the most fundamental quality of the Platonic/Socratic ethics. It is most explicitly stated in the *Philebus*.

---

[5] ibid., 30c9–30d2.

[6] "For I do nothing but go about persuading you all, old and young alike, not to take thought for your persons or your properties, but first and chiefly to care about the greatest achievement of the soul." ibid., 29d9–29e3.

The *Philebus* is an interesting dialogue for at least three reasons pertinent to this discussion. First, Socrates, as in the *Symposium*, distances himself from some of his most important contributions by attributing them to some other, divine source and claiming that he is only passing on knowledge he has learned from another. In the *Symposium* he credited Diotima for his theory of love[7], and here in *Philebus* Socrates calls the evidence for his assertions "a gift from the gods," and refers to "a theory that I heard long ago—I may have dreamed it."[8] Clearly there is some measure of Socratic irony to these deferences. Perhaps he is alluding to the fact that these theories were actually developed by Plato in the Academy, long after the historical Socrates of these dialogues asserted them. For the purpose here, his attempts at distancing himself from his words may appear to lend them the credence attached to ideas which are passed on rather than stumbled upon. These attempts also draw attention even more specifically to Socrates' unique method. Throughout what follows these instances of irony and their significance are brought to the surface, and in the following chapter an analogous Nietzschean style of ironic mockery is considered as well.

In the *Philebus*, as in the *Phaedrus*, Socrates displays his difficulty in committing himself to the one-sided worldview often assumed to be his. Initially in the *Phaedrus* it seems as if Socrates is arguing for the reasoned and dispassionate life, voicing support for this way of life in his reaction to Lysias' speech, and in the first of his own speeches. It is in his second, vastly superior speech that he diverges from what is commonly taken to be his position, supporting the necessity of unreasoned passion in the good life. This often overlooked aspect of Socratic thought, that reason alone is insufficient for a philosophic life, that it requires a certain measure of its opposite, passion, leads to the second Socratic imperative for right-living

---

[7] *Symposium*, 201d2.
[8] *Philebus*, 16c5 and 19b5 (Hackforth, trans.).

argued here. This second Socratic imperative, that passion and reason require and depend upon one another, is an important quality of Socrates' character. It is a quality which makes this Socrates much different from the Socrates of the harsh Plato of the *Republic*. Illustrating this argument is the main assertion of the dialogue *Philebus*, that the reasoned, intelligent life which Socrates defines in an important new way as the dialogue concludes, is superior to and more divine than the pleasure-seeking life favored by Philebus and Protarchus, the interlocutors. What this assertion comes to mean is a new and more sophisticated understanding of the life of reason, which becomes an imperative for whoever would want for himself the best possible life.

In the *Philebus* it appears as if Socrates is arguing for the primacy of "right opinion and true reasoning" over the physical, bodily pleasures, and for the most part he is.[9] His metaphysical argument here is consonant with that of the *Symposium* insofar as it rests on the distinction between the one and the many, just as his encomium of Eros rests on an ascension from many small and individual instances of love to a perception of the perfect form of love in which all the others participate. This aspect of the *Symposium* and its connection to a philosophy of everyday life is elaborated in greater detail below. As in that dialogue and many other places, here as well Socrates first adumbrates the majority opinion, then demonstrates where that opinion goes wrong, countering it with his own right opinion. Opposing the view of some of his contemporaries that the sum of the universe, though appearing to comprise many different elements, is in fact one, he warns, "So you mustn't put any faith in this argument that makes all sorts of absolutely opposite things into one thing."[10] Socrates'

---

[9] ibid., 11b8: "...but that thought, intelligence, memory, and things akin to these, right opinion and true reasoning, prove better and more valuable than pleasure for all such beings as can participate in them, and that for all these, whether now living or yet to be born, nothing in the world is more profitable than so to participate."

[10] ibid., 13a2.

own view as he presents it in this dialogue is more subtle than this. His admits of the one and the many, but suggests that the task of man is to examine a third category which attaches itself to things and is overlooked by most, the intermediary.

The way to truth is obscured for Philebus, Protarchus, and the many others of their opinion, because in examining only the one (for example, pleasure) and the many (the infinitely numerous instances of pleasurable experiences) they overlook the crucial middle ground, which necessarily limits the unlimited and thus facilitates human participation in the world. This is Socrates' "gift of the gods," alluded to above:"All things, so it ran, that are ever said to be consist of a one and a many, and have in their nature a conjunction of limit and unlimitedness." He continues, explaining,

> This then being the ordering of things we ought, they said, whatever it be that we are dealing with, to assume a single form and search for it, for we shall find it there contained, then, if we have laid hold of that, we must go on from one form to look for two, if the case admits of there being two, otherwise for three or some other number of forms. And we must do the same again.... But we are not to apply the character of unlimitedness to our plurality until we have discerned the total number of forms the thing in question has intermediate between its one and its unlimited number.[11]

This passage is confusing and worth quoting at length. Its primary implication is that pleasure can appear to be the ultimate good when its

---

[11] ibid., 16c10.This passage continues, "It is only then, when we have done that, that we may let each one of all these intermediate forms pass away into the unlimited and cease bothering about them." Socrates concludes by suggesting that this difficult task is the responsibility of the intellect, and much of his argument derives from this suggestion.This long and confounding passage is perhaps the most crucial to the substance of his argument in this dialogue.

nature is misunderstood, or perceived inaccurately. With pleasure, like with anything else, there is perfect pleasure, never to be attained by man, and innumerable day-to-day instances which are imperfect derivations from the perfect form. Understood in just this way, Philebus believes that the best thing that man can do is accumulate and enjoy as many pleasures as possible as often as possible, in an attempt to come as close as possible to perfect pleasure, which he intuits as the greatest good. For Socrates, Philebus' view amounts to a logical fallacy. Socrates, ironically attributing his contrary opinion to some unknown source or a long-ago dream, maintains that Philebus, though his opinion may be the more popular, suffers from a fundamental misunderstanding. Setting himself up for what is called here his second imperative for right-living, Socrates demonstrates the misunderstanding, and from it derives proof demonstrating intellect the greater good than pleasure, philosophy the greatest good.

Socrates shows Protarchus, by means of a number of different examples and devices, that the intellect rules all.[12] Even pleasure, Philebus' greatest good, could not exist without intellectual knowledge. Socrates observes of pleasure that "If you were without reason, memory, knowledge, and true judgment, you would necessarily, I imagine, in the first place be unaware even whether you were, or were not, enjoying yourself, as you would be destitute of all intelligence."[13] Here the movement of the argument is in three steps. First is the assumption that there exist intermediary instances between the one and the many which are accessible to the intellect. Socrates moves from this assumption to the belief that the intellect, when coming to bear on these intermediary instances, reveals truths previously concealed about the thing-in-itself as it exists in its perfect form. The conclusion is that when this reasoning is applied to the form of pleasure, it

---

[12] Socrates, "supports those ancient thinkers that we mentioned, who declared that reason always rules all things," ibid., 30d6.

[13] ibid., 21b5.

becomes clear that pleasure requires intelligence, so that intelligence must by definition be the greater good.

Yet there is more of significance to this theme of the dialogue than the relationship between pleasure and knowledge. Related to this theme, yet much greater in implication, is the contrast Socrates believes exists, between perfect being and what he calls becoming, or coming-to-pass and perishing:the transient quality of the world. Along with the assumed dichotomy between soul and body, this assumed dichotomy between being and becoming is a critical quality of Platonic/Socratic metaphysics. It clearly underlies Socratic ethics in significant ways, and leads to what is called here the third Socratic imperative. To attain to both the best earthly life and to ensure the success of the soul after death, becoming must be allowed to approach as closely as possible to being. This important theme is discussed at greater length below as it is crucial to Socrates' change of opinion in the *Phaedrus*, and the progression of his thought throughout that dialogue. The contrast between being and becoming is related to the primacy of knowledge over pleasure and introduced on its account, yet is of much wider significance.

Socrates argues that "pleasure is something that comes to be, but never is."[14] Pleasure is clearly situated within the category of coming to be and perishing, rather than that of enduring eternally and never changing. As such, pleasure would seem to be inferior to reason just as everything changing is inferior to what is eternal. But as the following reading argues, this is not so with pleasure. Pleasure proves to be a unique hybrid; everywhere accompanying the philosophic life as the philosopher reasons himself up from the many, through the intermediary, to the one in his contemplation of the good. Unlike truth, pleasure is never attained, even after death. Pleasure is inherently earthly, yet as necessary to the philosophic life as reason. Pleasure accompanies reason, allowing it a kind of

---

[14] ibid., 54d4.

self-awareness of when it is on the right path. Reason requires pleasure; requires its management in order to struggle successfully within its earthly constraints. Much of the argument that follows is concerned with the unique and often overlooked role of pleasure in Socratic thought, and how a new reading of that role helps limn a Socratic philosophy of everyday life.

Socrates derives ethical imperatives from his metaphysical assumptions. Pleasure lacks the perfection inherent in eternal, unchanging being. On the contrary, it is by definition of the number of lower order experiences, subject to change and imperfect. This idea of the *Philebus* seems to depart from while elaborating on a similar theme Socrates details in the *Symposium* during his encomium of Eros. This is the difficult idea of the relation among particular occurrences of love, the ascending movement to a more general love, appreciation and acceptance of perfect Love, and moreover this motion as an example of the movement from the imperfect becoming characterizing the human experience to the perfect being of which this interminable becoming can possibly remind us when approached in the right way.

These passages of the *Symposium* are worth considering with respect to Socrates' treatment of these themes in the *Philebus* and elsewhere. In his speech on love in the *Symposium* Socrates relates a theory on the nature of Eros he has learned, he tells Phaedrus and his other friends with his usual self-effacing and ironic modesty, from a foreign priestess called Diotima. Here we learn that it is she who has taught Socrates the doctrine crucial to the *Philebus* explicated above concerning the necessary intermediaries between the one and the many. In the *Symposium* this theme is introduced mainly as a framework within which the discussion of love develops, then in the *Philebus* Socrates imposes this framework on pleasure in order to demonstrate its inferiority to reason. Though in the *Philebus*, as explained below, Socrates expands his understanding of the ideas he puts forth in the *Symposium*, it is nevertheless interesting to examine the manner in which he develops his philosophy at the drinking party and the way in which this particular speech importantly anticipates his later thinking.

The participants in the *Symposium* agree to an erotic discussion, in which each person will offer a speech praising the god Eros, each speaker trying to outdo the one preceding him. The initial difficulty is that Eros appears to desire what is good and beautiful, yet if he were a god, as Socrates and Phaedrus maintain, finally, in the *Phaedrus*, discussed below, he would in virtue of his divine nature possess the good and the beautiful, and one by definition does not desire what one already possesses. The solution is that Eros is neither god nor mortal, but some intermediary thing "between mortal and immortal."[15] Diotima explains to Socrates what this combination entails for Eros, and consequently for human beings, and Socrates teaches that consistent with Eros' intermediary nature is that his knowledge and understanding exist tenuously between the perfect wisdom of the gods and the complete lack of understanding of the fool.

At the outset of her instruction Diotima has shown Socrates, "That to opine correctly without being able to give an account is neither to know expertly (for how could expert knowledge be an unaccounted for matter?) nor lack of understanding (for how could lack of understanding be that which has hit upon what is)? But surely correct opinion is like that, somewhere between intelligence and lack of understanding?"[16] Hidden here, as is so often the case, are at least two important ideas. First, there are not simply two extremes with respect to any virtue or vice, but an infinite middle ground between them wherein human life occurs. Further, the very pursuit to which Socrates himself has devoted the whole of his life, and for which he dies, is perhaps the best example of this fact.

---

[15] *Symposium*, 202c8.
[16] ibid., 202a5–202a10.

Right opinion is nothing other than discerning enough of truth, beauty, and the good to live well, while knowing that it remains impossible to give an account of why this right opinion is right. Here Diotima teaches Socrates something which is clearly of great importance to his way of life, comparable to his interpretation of the Delphic oracle recounted in the *Apology*. Diotima then derives from this observation her description of Eros, that

> His nature is neither immortal nor mortal; but sometimes on the same day he flourishes and lives, whenever he has resources; and sometimes he dies, but gets to live again through the nature of his father. And as that which is supplied to him is always gradually flowing out, Eros is never either without resources or wealthy, but is in between wisdom and lack of understanding.[17]

Here is the connection between Eros and philosophy. Eros is by definition a philosopher, knowing enough, much like Socrates, to seek what he knows he does not have.[18] The love of wisdom of the philosopher involves the pleasure that accompanies the search for knowledge. As the philosopher ascends in his search, new pleasures accompany new discoveries. But these pleasures are always coming to pass and changing. Though pleasure does not endure in the way of the searched after eternal truths; nevertheless it is necessary for that search, so long as it is confined to the earth.

Eros' nature is somewhere in between mortal and immortal. Yet, like mortals through procreation, Eros desires a kind of immortality.[19] Diotima first observes, "For in this way every mortal thing is preserved;

---

[17] ibid., 203e1–204a1.

[18] "For wisdom is one of the most beautiful things, and Eros is love in regard to the beautiful; and so Eros is—necessarily—a philosopher; and as a philosopher he is between being wise and being without understanding," ibid., 204b2–204b6.

[19] "This thing, pregnancy and bringing to birth, is divine, and it is immortal in the animal that is mortal," ibid., 206c7–206c9.

not by being absolutely the same forever, as the divine is, but by the fact that that which is departing and growing old leaves behind another young thing that is as it was."[20] The divine is more perfect insofar as it is perfect and endures perfectly unchanging. Mortals change through time and are therefore imperfect, changing, always coming to be and passing away. However, mortals approach immortality in an approximate way through procreation, as Diotima observes in the above quoted passage.

Diotima, and through her Socrates, bring together the metaphysical opposition of being and becoming in order to derive an ethical imperative for right-living. Eros approaches the perfection of the divine as closely as he can, in collusion with mankind and working through men to create works and deeds of beauty that will endure beyond the lives of those creating. Diotima prescribes for Socrates, and he in turn lives in this way and teaches it to others, a way of life allowing as much as humanly possible for the attainment of this end, immortality. Or, perhaps more accurately, a way of life which allows these immortal perfections to be most closely approached and understood by living mortals.

Diotima begins from an assumption of right-living, just as Socrates does so often. What she describes is a process that will come naturally to the virtuous man, but that will be unknown to or misunderstood by another, or certainly at least undervalued by him. A young man raised up virtuously will at some point come into contact with someone who will allow his nascent goodness to develop, and their friendship is the beginning of this individual's progress toward the understanding of perfect truth. Diotima describes the relationship of the educator to his pupil: "And to this human being he is at once fluent in speeches about virtue—of what sort the good man must be and what he must practice—and he tries to educate him."[21] Like so many of these passages, it is easy to read much

---

20 ibid., 208a3–208b1
21 ibid., 209d10–209e2.

irony into these chaste and altruistic descriptions, especially when considering as an example the personal relationship between Socrates and Alcibiades, which is elaborated in the *Symposium*, but alluded to in many other places as well, such as the *Protagoras*. Nevertheless, this feeling of irony is severely mitigated by the example of Socrates' own life:the unflagging virtuous living exhibited in his philosophic lifestyle. In this passage, then, is the first step the virtuous youth will take, even while he does not know he is taking it, toward the ultimate goal of the philosophic life. Discussing, as Socrates' own life exemplifies, the nature and practice of virtue; the interlocutor attempting to lead his friend and pupil out of himself in such a way that he is able to come to an understanding of an idea on his own.

The end of these conversations will be the development of the individual's faculty for seeking after and appreciating truth and beauty, though perhaps only in limited or individual instances. After this ability is attained, Diotima continues about the individual in question, "Then he must realize that the beauty that is in any body whatsoever is related to that in another body; and if he must pursue the beauty of looks, it is great folly not to believe that the beauty of all bodies is one and the same."[22] This is the second movement; from an appreciation of that first instance of truth and beauty to an understanding that it exists to be discovered in many other places also. But this cannot remain the final belief, because it too is incomplete and contains a misunderstanding. Implicit in the statement just quoted is that the beauty beheld and appreciated is merely a physical beauty; however, beauty is more truly a quality of the soul. Diotima is succinct, and as is always the case, the attic metaphysical primacy of the soul over the body is implicit:"After this he must believe that the beauty in souls is more honorable than that in the body."[23] This then is the three stage progression through which the virtuous man will almost

---

[22] ibid., 210a10–210b4.
[23] ibid., 210b8–210b9.

inevitably pass[24], and which is, according to Diotima and most likely also to Socrates, the purpose of human life.[25] The just and virtuous life, the pursuit of which leads a man ineluctably to as close an understanding as is available to him of the essence of truth, beauty, and the good.

In the *Symposium* Socrates has demonstrated what he believes is the goal of the good life:the pursuit of beauty to its natural end in its perfect form. The practice of philosophy is the best means available to the individual for approaching this end as closely as possible on earth, and for preparing the soul for the complete attainment of this end after death. Usually, as appears implicit in the *Symposium*, he argues for the importance of reason in the life of the good. And this often appears to be so even in the *Philebus*. But though this defense of reason is certainly made clear in the *Philebus*, there is an additional requirement for the good human life indicated by the conversations of that dialogue. It is this additional requirement that leads to the formulation that is called here the second Socratic imperative, concerning pleasure, passion, and madness as an element of reason.

As is so often the case, this aspect of Socratic philosophy is demonstrated both by the arguments and conversations, and by the manner in which they progress. In fact, despite the earnestness of his argument in the *Philebus*, and Plato is, in that dialogue as much as in any other of his later writings, at his most serious, his Socrates almost cannot help but allow for another, seemingly contrary viewpoint to that of the sole importance and lone necessity of reason. It is a small but significant admission. Socrates

---

[24] Diotima summarizes the process, teaching "For this is what it is to proceed correctly, or to be led by another, to erotics—beginning from these beautiful things here, always to proceed on up for the sake of that beauty, using these beautiful things here as steps:from one to two, and from two to all beautiful bodies; and from beautiful bodies to beautiful pursuits; and from pursuits to beautiful lessons; and from lessons to end at that lesson, which is the lesson of nothing else than the beautiful itself; and at last to know what is beauty itself" ibid., 211b10–211e10.

[25] ibid., 210e9–211c2.

says of his purpose in that dialogue, "What I wanted to discover at present, my dear Protarchus, was not which art or which form of knowledge is superior to all others in respect of being the greatest or the best or the most serviceable, but which devotes its attention to precision, exactness, and the fullest truth, though it may be small and of small profit."[26] Socrates is not concerned for utility or personal or communal benefit but merely for whatever small but certain truth for right-living he can discover or figure out by means of the discussion.

Socrates believes in the seriousness of his task, concluding the above mentioned paragraph, "But if there is a certain faculty in our souls naturally directed to loving truth and doing all for the sake of truth, let us make diligent search and say what it is."[27] And yet, well-concealed among the rhetoric of small but certain truth, eternal being instead of transient pleasure, the primacy of the faculty of reason and the ruling intellect, there is the acknowledgment that even the most rigorous searching for knowledge is in need of moderate pleasures to keep in check. Socrates suggests that there are in fact "true and pure" pleasures, saying that, "the pleasures you have spoken of as pure and true you may regard as more or less related to us, and besides them you may add to the mixture those that consort with health and temperance, and in fact all that attend upon virtue in general, following her everywhere as their divinity."[28] Certain pleasures play a part in the good life, as it has been determined to mean a life of reason and knowledge, so long as it is reason that accepts responsibility for moderating these pleasures. Whereas in the *Phaedo* Socrates' apparent attack on pleasure is actually only against bodily pleasures, in the *Phaedrus* and the *Philebus* he expands his definition of pleasure in such a way, as hinted at even in the *Symposium*, as to make it crucial to a life of reason. This aspect

---

[26] *Philebus.*, 58b7.
[27] ibid., 58d7.
[28] ibid., 63e2.

of Socrates' philosophy is in fact elaborated much more generously in Plato's *Phaedrus*, and informs Nietzsche's attack on Socrates in *Twilight of the Idols*, which will be discussed further in the following chapter.

The *Phaedrus* is much different from *Philebus*, especially with respect to its style. It is a dialogue which is noteworthy with respect to both its dramatic and intriguing writing and its philosophic content, whereas in the *Philebus* what is most noticeable is the latter, and in many of the earlier, aporetic dialogues, the former. In the *Symposium* Socrates' individuality is evident in many places. From the very beginning when he falls behind Aristodemus and, as Aristodemus arrives at Agathon's home, Socrates remains standing outside gazing at the heavens, until the end when, unaffected by the wine, he puts his friends to sleep and returns to the marketplace to go about his daily business. And throughout that dialogue the unique nature of Socrates is revealed, both through and in addition to Plato's philosophy.

Similarly in the *Phaedrus* the reader sees Socrates at his very best, strolling barefoot outside the city limits with his young friend who is also, though it is not his usual custom, barefoot. They choose a pleasant spot to rest and converse, and the conversation is very cordial, without the earnestness of the *Philebus* while concerned with many of the same themes as both the *Philebus* and the *Symposium*. However, like the *Philebus* the discussion produces an interesting and important idea concerning the role of passion in the reasoned life, which is important to consider here as it illuminates the significance of this Socratic imperative. In fact, the *Phaedrus* is a bold dialogue insofar as it deals with a number of important issues. Initially it seems like the discussion will concern the motives of those in love, whether they are looking out for themselves or for their beloved, and whether the beloved is better served consorting with one who loves him or one indifferent. Socrates seems pleased to have met up with Phaedrus, and wants Phaedrus to declaim for him a speech of Lysias' which Phaedrus has just heard and of which he possesses a copy. This part of the dialogue seems typical of Socratic irony, as the reader is aware that Socrates values speech over writing, as he makes explicit at the end of this dialogue but also because he devoted his life to conversing rather than writing. This irony indicates that what is about to proceed in the dialogue may be more complex than it will seem at first blush. The twofold significance so far is the subject matter of the speech and the form of Lysias' opinion as a written text. The dialogue begins with Socrates' learning from Phaedrus that Lysias supports the position that the beloved should choose the nonlover over the lover. This position is in keeping with a belief in the primacy of reason over passion. Socrates learns from Phaedrus that Lysias defends his view by means of a number of observations and assertions all of which derive from a very negative notion of love.

Lysias regards love as a sickness, and wants to affirm reason, the domain of the nonlover, over passion, the cause of the bad judgment and poor character of the lover. This seems to accord with what is often considered, including by Nietzsche as seen in the following chapter, the Socratic primacy of reason. Yet Lysias says of himself, "I am the master of myself, rather than the victim of love," making love out to be an evil.[29] Already this is a strong indication that Socrates will not be able to support this view, even if at first he seems to, because clearly what Lysias means by "master" conflicts with what Socrates means by "self-mastery" or "self-control," lending credence to reading Socrates' initial support of Lysias' position as vintage Socratic irony. Lysias stresses the importance of public and family opinion, contrary to Socrates' opinion in the *Crito* and elsewhere, noting that "a lover is bound to be heard about and seen by many people, consorting with his beloved and caring about little else, so that when they are observed talking to one another, the meeting is taken to imply the satisfaction, actual or prospective, of their desires."[30] Lysias believes that the beloved should avoid the company of a lover on account

---

[29] *Phaedrus*, 233c1 (Hackforth, trans.).
[30] ibid., 232a8.

of the opprobrium of the public, and, as he continues, of their families:"Lovers are admonished by their friends and relatives for the wrongness of their conduct."[31] Lysias' view is consistently negative toward love and passion, and overly sensitive to the perceptions and opinions of the masses rather than to the individuals involved. Nevertheless and contrary to what a listener might expect, Socrates at first accepts and offers further arguments for Lysias' viewpoint.

As in so many other places, Socrates feigns irresponsibility for what he is about to say, attributing his words to "the wise men and women who in past ages have spoken and written on this theme...the fair Sappho maybe, or the wise Anacreon, or perhaps some prose writer."[32] What Socrates takes issue with in Lysias' speech is the actual writing itself, its style and technique; not the substance of his argument so much as its method. This is an idea he returns to at the close of the dialogue, in his discursion on language. Here he asks if "as regards the subject of the speech, do you imagine that anybody could argue that the non-lover should be favored, rather than the lover, without praising the wisdom of the one and censuring the folly of the other?"[33] Socrates agrees with Lysias' position, and attempts to offer a better speech in praise of that position. The shocking divergence this would mean from his usual position hints that Socrates is ironically demonstrating, even before he begins his two speeches, that Lysias is not to be taken seriously, and that Socrates will demonstrate why, both by a recapitulation of Lysias' own speech, and by a new and uniquely Socratic speech. Both of Socrates' speeches point out an important Socratic ethical imperative for right-living, the redefining of reason to account for the necessity of passion.

Socrates begins the first of his two speeches with the suggestion of a metaphysical principle that the soul contains and is motivated by two

---

[31] ibid., 234b2.

[32] ibid., 235b7.

[33] ibid., 235e6.

principles, sometimes in accord and sometimes contrary, an "innate desire for pleasure" and "acquired judgment."[34] Based on this idea of a bipartite composition of the soul, Socrates is able to define love in this disturbing and unlikely way:"When irrational desire, pursuing the enjoyment of beauty, has gained the mastery over judgment that prompts to right conduct, and has acquired from other desires, akin to it, fresh strength to strain toward bodily beauty, that very strength provides it with its name—it is the strong passion called love."[35] There is a lot going on in this bizarre yet interesting passage. Desire and the irrational are connected and set in opposition to judgment and right-living, and love is defined as the mastery within an individual of the former over the latter. Once again, this notion of mastery seems much different than the virtue of self-mastery. In this passage Socrates appears to value reason over passion. He condemns passion just as Lysias has before him, simply attempting to do so through more pleasing oratory.

Fortunately Socrates is not long in realizing the error in his thinking. As he and Phaedrus are about to part company, going their separate ways and considering the discussion concluded, Socrates experiences a sudden realization. His familiar divine sign, the same one that reassured him of his decisions in the *Apology* and elsewhere, and which itself is an example from his own life of his philosophic imperative that reason requires divine madness, visits him. Socrates realizes that he has gone astray and must at once atone: "At the moment when I was about to cross the river, dear friend, there came to me my familiar divine sign—which always checks me when on the point of doing something or other—and all at once I seemed to hear a voice, forbidding me to leave the spot until I had made atonement for some offense to heaven."[36] Socrates realizes that Lysias' belief that the nonlover is more virtuous than the lover is misguided for at

---

[34] ibid., 237d2–238b5.

[35] ibid., 238d9.

[36] ibid., 242b9.

least one reason, and from that reason, so important to his encomium of divine Eros in the *Symposium*, he determines a new perspective in defense of which he will deliver a new speech. As Socrates notices, "If Love is, as he is indeed, a god or a divine being, he cannot be an evil thing; yet this pair of speeches treated him as evil."[37] Socrates reconsiders his position, stating that "Other things being equal, favor should be accorded to the lover rather than the nonlover."[38] It is from the assumption of the divinity of Eros that he begins his new speech.

As with his initial speech, Socrates does not take credit for this second effort. Rather, with his usual ironic modesty he attributes it to Stesichorus.[39] It is at this point in the *Phaedrus* where Socrates is at his artistic best. Socrates' new premise is how best to allow the divine to become accessible to the human; an aspect of his metaphysics which clearly informs the development of his ethical imperatives. He returns to an idea which occurs continually and significantly in his dialogues:the greater importance of that which always is over that which comes to be and perishes; or, being over becoming. Just as in the *Philebus*, this notion is critical to Socrates' main argument in the *Phaedrus*. There is an interconnectedness of the metaphysical and the ethical, and a further but related connection between what are called here the second and third Socratic imperatives. The assumption that eternal and unchanging being undergirds the ever-changing and imperfect human life leads Socrates to the observation that man requires in his life, if he wants to ascend as close as he can to the divine, both the practice of reason and the divine gift of madness. In this way these three facets of Socrates' second speech come to bear on his definition of love:unchanging being; the virtue of reason; divine madness, passion, and love.

---

[37] ibid., 242e2.

[38] ibid., 243d8.

[39] "That which I shall now pronounce is by Stesichorus, son of Euphemus, of Himera," ibid., 244a2.

In the second speech of this dialogue Socrates offers a greatly detailed description of the nature of eternal things. The bulk of this second speech is devoted to describing how the immortal soul moves from its earthly body to heaven and back again, and the difference between its existence in heaven and on earth. In heaven the soul perceives all manner of perfections, while on earth it is distracted and limited on account of its somatic imprisonment. But the soul's time on earth affects its future in heaven, by either preparing properly for its ascension through the practice of philosophy or hindering its ascension through too excessive enjoyment of bodily pleasures. The human being must exercise reason to keep his soul in check and best prepare it for ascension to the heavens. This is the importance of reason to human life which is characterized by the practice of philosophy. This is an important theme of the *Phaedo* as well, and the contribution of that dialogue to this idea is considered in detail below.

In the *Phaedrus* Socrates explains the idea of the conflict between reason and passion in human life through his well-known metaphor of the soul as a charioteer driving two steeds; one noble, the other wayward. In this passage he appears to value reason first while acknowledging passion's important role. He employs this metaphor to illuminate the difference between the nature of the human soul and the nature of the divine, suggesting of the soul,

> Let it be likened to the union of powers in a team of winged steeds and their winged charioteer. Now all the gods' steeds and all their charioteers are good, and of good stock, but with other beings it is not wholly so. With us men, in the first place, it is a pair of steeds that the charioteer controls; moreover one of them is noble and good and of good stock, while the other has the opposite character, and his stock is opposite. Hence the task of our charioteer is difficult and troublesome.[40]

---

[40] ibid., 246a6.

Toward the end of his speech he returns to this image, describing the nature of the good as opposed to the bad steed, and the reactions of the steeds to earthly temptation and the difficulty of the charioteer in restraining the bad one.[41] The significance of the image is that it demonstrates the importance of reason, and related qualities such as judgment, temperance, and self-control to the good human life. And the need of these qualities to keep in check the natural but contrary urges of the body toward its own bodily pleasures. In fact, this is how the philosophy and lifestyle of Socrates is commonly perceived, and with good reason. Bodily needs weigh an individual down; philosophical practices divest the soul of its dependence on the body, improving its ability to ascend to the realm of the forms after death. However, as adumbrated above and argued more explicitly below, this may not be the complete picture.

In understanding the issue of the relationship between the human body and its soul it is instructive to consider some passages of the *Phaedo*. The *Phaedo* is important to this discussion because in it Socrates deals at great length with his most primary philosophical questions:what is the relationship of the soul to the body during life; and what is the nature of the soul's immortality after death. In the *Phaedo* Socrates discusses the nature of the human soul and describes why some ways of life are more conducive than others to the soul's well-being while on earth and to its ability to ascend to the realm of the forms after its separation from the body in death.

The *Phaedo* reveals much of significance about the nature of the human soul and the relationship between soul and body. Conclusions similar to those of the *Philebus* but more narrow than those of the *Phaedrus* are reached, though in different ways. Contrary to Alcibiades' assertion that Socrates is always saying the same things through the same things, in the *Phaedo* he deploys a number of unique metaphors in describing the soul and its nature, and derives from these his prescription

---

[41] ibid., 253c6–255a1.

for what he considers right-living in human life. Socrates sets the tone for the discussion to follow by observing how

> Ordinary people seem not to realize that those who really apply themselves in the right way to philosophy are directly and of their own accord preparing themselves for dying and death. If this is true, and they have actually been looking forward to death all their lives, it would of course be absurd to be troubled when the thing comes for which they have so long been preparing and looking forward.[42]

Socrates believes, as this passage and so many others make abundantly clear, that the practice of philosophy provides the very best way for a man to live his life. Additionally, it is the best way for a man to prepare himself for his inevitable movement to the next world. This is not an arbitrary belief, but one at which he arrives through an honest and logical consideration of all he observes and knows of human life. It is also the belief which is so abhorrent to Nietzsche.

In the *Phaedo* Socrates begins from the assumption of the dualism between soul and body, and the primacy of the divine-like soul over and in opposition to the inherent deceptions of the body. He observes how in the course of an individual's pursuit of knowledge, "Surely the soul can best reflect when it is free of all distractions such as hearing or sight or pain or pleasure of any kind—that is, when it ignores the body and becomes as far as possible independent, avoiding all physical contacts and associations as much as it can, in its search for reality."[43] At this point, pleasure is connected only with what is bodily and not yet with the process of philosophic introspection. For Socrates the body, its sense perceptions, and the feeling of pleasure are only impediments to the search for knowledge and truth, providing an introspective and reflective soul with only misleading

---

[42] Phaedo, 64a4–64a9 (Tredennick, trans.).

[43] ibid., 65e3–65e6.

distractions. Reality is not what the bodily perceptions sense, a metaphysical position opposed and reversed by Nietzsche. The human being in pursuit of the most true knowledge available to him must avoid distracting physical perceptions while concentrating his attentions on matters of understanding and the soul.

This is a concept crucial to the most central assertions of the *Republic*. Throughout the *Republic* and connected to all of the different ideas discussed there is the underlying tension between truth and appearance. For Socrates, the practice of philosophy is the direction of human life at every turn toward the search for truth. But he observes that contrary to his view, the vast majority prefer the comfort of the world of appearance instead. Although elsewhere Socrates acknowledges other ways to knowledge and truth, in the *Republic* he maintains that reason alone is the means to truth. Even sense perceptions are deceptive, and Socrates warns his listeners about,"so-called pleasures that reach the soul through the body."[44] True knowledge is attained through reason alone, only the appearance of knowledge is arrived at through the senses. This appearance is what Socrates refers to as opinion intwo well-known and important images:the divided line, each segment representing an ascension toward truth; and the cave with its prisoners and shadowy images of reality.

The significance of the divided line is that it represents, like the descriptions of the *Symposium* and the *Phaedo*, the ascension from false opinion to true opinion to knowledge and truth. Whereas in those dialogues Socrates is concerned with the movement from an appreciation of individual instances of beauty, to an understanding of perfect beauty itself, throughout the *Republic* and here in particular he is occupied with the movement from always-changing sense perceptions to opinion and then upwards to unchanging truths, discerned solely through the faculty of reason. The prisoners of the cave only know the light of the fire behind them,

---

[44] Republic, 584c3.

they do not know of the existence of the sun. They know only the shadowy figures on the wall in front of them, they do not know the real objects reflecting those figures. When one among them flees the cave into the sunlight, surely the others will not believe his accounts. When the philosopher lives so as to prepare himself for his soul's ascension from earthly approximations to eternal truths, Socrates expects that he will be misunderstood and feared. When his life yields prescriptions which are beneficial regardless of the eternal fate of the soul, his influence may be more widely applicable than even he had hoped.

Perhaps the most important characteristic of the philosophic man is self-control, or self-mastery and temperance. That is, the practiced ability to overcome the body's impulses toward taking pleasure in the many earthly delights. Socrates offers a suggestion to the soul's charioteer for reigning in the wayward steed and subjugating him to his more noble companion, to refer back to that image from the *Phaedrus*. Socrates defines this most important virtue by saying that "Self-control, too, as it is understood even in the popular sense—not being carried away by the desires, but preserving a decent indifference toward them—is not this appropriate only to those who regard the body with the greatest indifference and spend their lives in philosophy?"[45] This is both Socrates' recommendation for the best possible human life, and the way he attempts to live his own life. As his life reaches its conclusion, these beliefs allow him to die contentedly.

Socrates believes that deleterious human habitsare overcome through the practice of right-reason; that in this way human life can most closely approach the divine, and the soul can be prepared for its separation from the body. This is a theme of both the *Phaedo* and the *Phaedrus*. But in the *Phaedrus* there is an additional and critical allowance for the importance of thinking unreasonably. It would be true, for example as asserted in the

---

[45] Phaedo, 68c6–68c10.

first two speeches of the *Phaedrus*, that the nonlover should be favored over the lover, if reason, the method of the former, were always preferable to madness, the quality of the latter. Here it is almost as if the lover and the nonlover were metaphors for passion and reason, respectively, and as if the dialogue were never dealing with love, or mere love, at all, but always with the greater, though inclusive, issue of the contradictory responsibilities of passion and reason in human life.

Socrates' new perspective, which he introduces in his second speech of the *Phaedrus* and which becomes the second imperative considered here for attaining the good life, is that "in reality, the greatest blessings come by way of madness, indeed of madness that is heaven-sent."[46] He cites a number of examples from mythology and his own epoch supporting his new view, and describes a number of different manifestations of madness, of which the love of the lover for his beloved is one. It is important to observe how this is not a reversal of his earlier opinion, but an allowance that it was incomplete, and incomplete in such an important way as to be an affront to the gods. Reason is still necessary for the good life, but alone is insufficient. From time to time it must relinquish its rule of the soul to passion, in order that passion may open the soul to ideas and feelings and experiences it never would otherwise have known, and that allow it to improve itself. Reason and passion inform the soul in tandem, the latter just as necessary as the former, the soul in need of both.

If his artistic best in the *Phaedrus* was his second speech on love, it is in his discussion of language which concludes that dialogue where Plato is at his most powerfully philosophical. Socrates critiques his and Lysias' speeches, summarizes his main points, then segues into a discussion on the nature of speaking and writing. There is much going on in this last part of the *Phaedrus*. Of concern here is the relation among truth, madness, and language Socrates discerns and puts forward at this point in the dialogue.

---

[46] *Phaedrus*, 244a7.

The conclusions he draws reaffirm those he drew from the earlier parts of the discussion, but approach them in a different and more general way.

For the majority, Socrates believes, speaking is for the purpose of persuasion, even at the expense of truth; he however believes that speaking is a means of arriving at the truth. Socrates describes the majority opinion on speaking in this way:

> There is, they maintain, absolutely no need for the budding orator to concern himself with the truth about what is just or good conduct, nor indeed about who are the just and good men whether by nature or education. In the law courts nobody cares a rap for the truth about these matters, but only about what is plausible.... Even actual facts ought sometimes not be stated.... And...say good-by to the truth forever.[47]

This is a quite prescient observation, considering the grievous injustice of his own trial, recounted in his *Apology*, or perhaps it is a rhetorical device of Plato's to contribute to the narrative quality of the dialogues as a whole. This passage points to a pertinent aspect of Socrates' beliefs:whereas the mass of people misuse the art of speaking for their own vicious purposes, Socrates advocates speech that is "pleasing to the gods."[48] It is pleasing because rather than more greatly obscure the truth while furthering some other, lesser end, it attempts to get closer to the truth.

Socrates believes that the art of speaking is superior to the art of writing. It is no coincidence that Socrates never wrote anything down, but devoted his life to conversation. He believes that conversing is a better way to arrive at truth, and he suggests some compelling reasons in support of this seemingly, especially now, counterintuitive belief. Once again Socrates attributes his opinion to another source, this time, like in the *Philebus*, to

---

[47] ibid., 272d4.
[48] ibid., 273e7.

ancient Egyptian mythology. Socrates says of the art of writing that "It is no true wisdom you offer your disciples, but only its semblance, for by telling them of many things without teaching them you will make them seem to know much, while for the most part they know nothing, and as men filled, not with wisdom, but with the conceit of wisdom, they will be a burden to their fellows."[49] This is a powerful sentence, with many implications and alluding to many different passages in Plato's dialogues and times in Socrates' life.

The contrast between the appearance of truth and truth itself is a theme of singular importance in the dialogues. Socrates' belief in truth leads to his death sentence and to his dignified acceptance of that sentence. Another important implication of this passage is the way Socrates redevelops his perspective as his end nears. In the *Phaedo* Socrates is suddenly composing and writing down poetry, just in case this is what a certain dream of his has been exhorting him to do instead of his usual practice of philosophy. However, the action of that dialogue itself seems to indicate that Socrates continues his belief in the importance of philosophy and discourse even up until the very end. In the *Phaedrus* Socrates suggests that by definition the written word cannot contain "important truth of permanent validity," and despite what he may say in the *Phaedo*, his conduct in that dialogue as in the others seems to reaffirm his belief in the importance of the philosophic life.[50]

Socrates' fear that clever speaking allows falsehood and persuasion to masquerade as truth is reminiscent of Glaucon's well-stated concern in the *Republic* that perfect injustice will by definition appear to be justice while perfect justice is anonymous and indiscernible. Glaucon suggests that no one would willingly practice justice instead of injustice. As in the *Phaedrus*, early in the *Republic* Socrates supports the pursuit of truth and virtue at any cost over any other, seemingly better pursuit, including the

---

[49] ibid., 275a7.
[50] ibid., 277d8.

appearance of truth and virtue. Yet despite this, for the reader who has grown to feel for and agree along with Socrates, the *Republic* can be a troubling and unsettling dialogue. Although Socrates continues to put forth many of his same ideas in the hypothetical city he is positing in this dialogue, he appears willing to pay a prohibitive price for them, the price of human freedom and consequently the best that humanity can accomplish in and through that freedom. In terms of the matters under examination here, it is worth considering the ways in which the Socrates of the *Republic* is consistent with the Socrates of the other dialogues, and the important ways in which he diverges. These considerations help further illuminate the Socratic imperatives for right-living.

Glaucon offers this extreme and challenging hypothesis as a point of departure for considering the opposition of injustice and justice at the outset of the *Republic*:

> ...the extreme injustice is to be thought just when one is not. So we must grant to the perfectly unjust perfect injustice and take nothing away; but we must allow the one who does the greatest wrongs to get the greatest fame for justice, and to recover if he does make a slip...let us in our theory set against him the just; a man simple and generous, one who wishes not to seem good but to be good, as Aeschylus says....He must be stripped naked of all but justice and made the opposite of the former; doing no wrong, let him have the greatest possible repute of injustice, that he may be tested for justice through not being softened by infamy and all that comes from it.[51]

This is a powerful suggestion from Glaucon, forcing Socrates' hand in the discussion. Glaucon burdens Socrates with the task of proving the value of justice over injustice in the extreme yet easily conceivable circumstance of injustice masquerading as justice while true justice goes

---

[51] *Republic*, 361a3–361c10.

unnoticed and unappreciated. This is a more tangible example of the situation described at the conclusion of the *Phaedrus*, concerning the dangerous fact that compelling speech or writing can more easily persuade to falsehood than truth from discourse can edify, enlighten, or educate.

Socrates observes that just as pleasure requires intellect, as he has demonstrated in the *Philebus*, so even injustice requires justice. At least implicitly, then, justice is more perfect than injustice in the same way that reason is more perfect than pleasure. Socrates asks of Thrasymachus regarding injustice, "Do you think a city, or an army, or a gang of robbers or thieves, or any other body of men that set out for some unjust purpose in common would be able to achieve their object if they dealt unjustly with each other?"[52] Even in a city, the main concern of the *Republic*, nothing but chaos will come from the practice of injustice. Even the unjust require an assumption of or superficial belief in justice, against which their clever and practiced injustice may provide them with advantages. If the unjust are able to accomplish anything at all, no matter how small, it is only because there is some justice in themselves or their activities. Socrates observes:

> Now when we say that the just are shown to be wiser and better and more able to act effectively, and the unjust to be incapable of accomplishing anything together, and when on the other hand we add that in fact those who do accomplish something with strong united action are sometimes unjust people—then we are not saying what is wholly true; for they could not have kept their hands off each other if they were absolutely unjust; it is clear that some justice was in them, which kept them from wronging each other as well as those they attacked, and by this justice they accomplished as much as they did.[53]

---

[52] ibid., 351c6–351c9.
[53] ibid., 352b6–352c6.

What is important and also most clear from this and the previous, related passage is the primary importance of justice in human life, even the unjust life. Yet there is something else going on in these passages which is related to Socrates' motivations elsewhere in the dialogues, but which leads him in a much different, almost contrary direction in the *Republic*.

If one were to read these passages contemporaneously with the *Apology* or the *Symposium*, or especially the *Phaedrus*, one would interpret this Socrates as identifying here as he does in those dialogues the most intrinsic and undeniable qualities of human life and existence. Socrates is acknowledging that even in the most unjust despot there is justice, and whatever little he accomplishes, even merely living from one day to the next, he accomplishes only on account of his small but crucial sense of justice. Socrates, the reader believes, is discovering and bringing to light human value where no one else would be able to discern it. Unfortunately, this is clearly not the whole truth of Socrates' position in the *Republic*. In much of this dialogue he advances opinions and theories which are terribly counter to his revelations and assertions in the other dialogues discussed here, and his logic in this one is not so compelling. Rather, one is suddenly saddened on Socrates' behalf.

Although he appears in one respect to accord all individuals some basic human worth, there are many more contrary examples throughout the dialogue in which he does the exact opposite. He often assumes a complete lack of human worth in the vast majority of individuals. This is a harsh statement, but there are far too many instances of it for the reader to overlook this aspect of his thought. Early in the dialogue he makes certain to set his harsh tone. Socrates' rhetorical method in this dialogue is to make analogies of the larger, the city, to the smaller, the individual, and also from the individual to the city. He also makes analogies from one art or practice to another in hopes of illuminating a more difficult idea by means of a more accessible one. For example, in one particular passage he is discussing medicine and justice. Socrates asks of Glaucon, expecting and receiving an enthusiastically positive response,

Then the healing art such as we described it, coupled with the art of dispensing justice in this fashion, you will ordain by law in the city; these will care for those of the people who are naturally good in body and soul, but if any are not, those who are not so in body they will leave to die, and those who are naturally bad in soul and incurable they will certainly themselves put to death?[54]

Socrates is clearly pursuing in his folly of attempting to extricate from the individual in terms of his nature and from the city in terms of its citizens any ills or evils. Yet this is an inherently futile and dangerous task for at least two reasons. The main reason is the substance of what is alluded to above, the implicit negation of inherent human worth and value. Another reason is the lack of appreciation of both human and urban complexity. Without any one small facet of its nature, the individual or the city would be completely different from what it is. Perhaps better, probably worse. What Socrates perceives as requiring extrication could just as well be necessary for the very best that an individual or a community can accomplish. This significant fact, though overlooked by Socrates, is quite extensively taken into account by Nietzsche, whose variations on this and other Socratic ideas are considered in the following chapter.

In the above passage Socrates takes an unwavering position against the sick, dying, and wayward. Just as a physician must allow an incurable man to die, so the state must actively seek out and destroy citizens possessing potentially harmful natures. Socrates is equally stringent with citizens permitted to live, in allotting to them even when they are still children what will be their lot in life. He introduces his "necessary lie," the myth he will teach the first generation of citizens, which they will then pass on as truth to subsequent generations.[55] Children who diverge even slightly from

---

54 ibid., 409e4–410a3.

55 "'So you are all brothers in the city,' we shall tell them in our fable, 'but while God molded you, he mingled gold in the generation of some and those are the ones fit to rule, who are therefore the most precious; he mingled silver in the assistants; and iron and brass in the farmers and the craftsmen....'" ibid., 415a2–415b1

Socrates' demanding expectations will not be allowed to improve with age, nor certainly to achieve their own kind of successes in their own ways, thereby disproving Socrates' hypothesis. He explains, "If any child of theirs has a touch of brass or iron, they will not be merciful to him on any account, but they will give him the value proper to his nature...."[56] Once again, as in the example above, Socrates displays a facet of his nature that is contrary to his behaviors and speeches in all of the other dialogues. It is a facet that is so rigid and hardhearted it almost seems evil.

Further, Socrates once again takes up a position like Lysias' in the *Phaedrus*. However, whereas in that dialogue he later recants his position and reproaches both Lysias and himself, in the *Republic* he continues from where he left off in his initial speech of the *Phaedrus*, and goes to even greater lengths to oppose love, passion, and freedom. It is here in the *Republic* that Socrates makes his well-known and shockingly counterintuitive case for censorship of poetry and music. Socrates is aware of the great power of art, and fearful that it might misinstruct the citizens by providing them imperfect examples for emulation. He wants propaganda as education and fears the unrestrainable power in art. Socrates admonishes, "We should rightly do away with the dirges of famous men,"[57] fearing a bad example for the men of his city, and is equally opposed to laughter, "They must not be too fond of laughter."[58] His assumption is correct. Art is powerful and moving, and presents its audience with ideas and perspectives they might not otherwise learn. Yet he underestimates the individual's ability to synthesize works of art in his own mind, and bring them to bear on his own life. Socrates has this to say about his artists,

> I believe we are about to say that poets and storytellers are wrong about men in the most important matters. They declare that

---

[56] ibid., 415b10–415c3.

[57] ibid., 387e9.

[58] ibid., 388e6.

many men are happy though unjust, and wretched although just; that injustice is profitable, if not found out, and justice good for others but plain loss for oneself. Such things we will forbid them to say, and command them to sing and to fable the opposite, don't you agree with me?[59]

It is not enough for the just man to know the value of justice. To disseminate this right opinion more widely, the art and poetry of the people must support this and only this idea. Socrates does not believe that his citizens could discern truths from works of art which appear to assert falsehoods, even though that is clearly his own relation to Homer, on whom he relies heavily, even in his attacks against Homer.

As he is against poetry, he is against the divine madness he ultimately supported in the *Phaedrus*. Here he repeats almost verbatim the opinion he was most against in that dialogue, saying about the laws in his city governing the relationship between a lover and his beloved, "A lover may kiss his beloved, and be with him and touch him, as his own son, for the grace of the beautiful, and with his consent; in all else, if he cares for anyone, he should be careful to behave in associating with him so that there shall never be a suspicion of anything more intimate than this, or if there is, he will have the blame of bad education and bad taste."[60] Socrates clearly values public perception and opinion over truth, whereas in the *Phaedrus*, and certainly in the *Apology* and the *Crito*, he maintained just the opposite. In the *Phaedrus* Socrates determines that the best gifts that come to man come through divinely inspired madness. These gifts include poetry, which he rails against here, and the love of the lover for his beloved, the expression of which he has just forbidden in his hypothetical city.

Socrates is much different in the *Republic* than he is in any of Plato's other dialogues. At first he seems at least homologous with his other incarnations, intimating the universal worth of all human beings in his

---

[59] ibid., 392a10–392b7.
[60] ibid., 403b5–403c2.

appreciation of the at least inchoate justice that exists in everyone. But then he moves suddenly and implacably in completely another direction. He seems to deny the idea of inherent human worth, and certainly the possibility of individual change or progress, or of the validity of different values from one person to the next. He is against the pursuits he has been most for, poetry and love and freedom to live well. He seems a different Socrates. Yet despite all this there is clearly a sense in which Socrates remains consistent with his best self even when he as at his worst, as he is in certain places in the *Republic*. Discussing the guardianship of his city, Socrates suggests that "We must choose out of the guardians men such as those whom we observe to be most careful for us all their lives long; who do with all their hearts whatever they think will be for the advantage of the city, and would in no way ever wish to do what is not."[61] What Socrates describes for his ideal city is a code of behavior he has already adopted for himself, as evidenced by his respect for his accusers in the *Apology*, his refusal of Crito's offer to bribe him out of prison in that eponymous dialogue, and his dignified drinking of the poison in the *Phaedo*. The consistency of Socrates' teachings in this passage and his actions in those other dialogues evidence his belief in a lived philosophy.

Another important consistency between the *Republic* and the other dialogues under consideration is Socrates' definition of the soul and the derivation from this definition of the means to the best living an individual can attain. In the *Phaedrus* Socrates has demonstrated the tripartite nature of the soul, one part straining toward pleasure, another noble part, and a third part keeping the other two in check. Socrates describes the soul similarly in the *Republic*, though relying less on metaphor and more on example and analogy, in keeping with the rhetorical device of the *Republic* of moving from the individual to the larger community, and then again to the individual. "There is," says Socrates, "in the man himself something about the soul which is better, and something which is worse, and when

---

[61] ibid., 412d8–412e2.

the naturally better masters the worse, they speak of 'stronger than him-self.'"[62] Socrates is speaking of self-control, or self-mastery; the individual's reigning in of his many contrary and contradictory desires, and subjugat-ing them to what is best in himself. This is an important underlying theme in the Socratic dialogues, and an idea that is often taken up in philosophy. Nietzsche especially takes up and expounds on this idea. His variations are considered in the following chapter.

Socrates becomes even more explicit than this in his discussion of the tripartite division of the soul in the *Republic*. In discussing the two initially more obvious of the three parts, he says, "Then we shall claim not unrea-sonably that these are two separate things and different from each other, calling the part of the soul with which it reasons the 'reasoning' part, and that by which it loves and hungers and thirsts, and is all aflutter about the other desires, the 'unreasoning' and 'desiring' part, a comrade of repletions and pleasures."[63] The latter part attuned to the physical pleasures, the for-mer to the pleasures of the intellect, just as in the *Phaedrus* and the *Philebus*, as seen above. The further consistency here in the *Republic* is the introduction of a third part of the soul, acting as a sort of mediator between these two parts, reproaching the individual for allowing too great license to the one part, and fortifying him for the more difficult but greater pleasures available when he may cultivate the more noble part. In this dialogue Socrates calls this faculty of the soul "temper," and says of it:"When desires force one contrary to reason, we see the man reproaching himself, and angry with what is forcing him within himself; we see some-thing like two warring factions within such a man, and the temper as an ally to the reason."[64] Although Socrates is more general and less metaphor-ical here than he is when discussing similar ideas elsewhere, nevertheless he clearly sees the soul as a complex of desires requiring proper ordering so

---

62 ibid., 431a5–435a8.

63 ibid., 439d4–439d10.

64 ibid., 440a10–440b3.

that the individual may be able to live well and freely, and not become enslaved to his more base desires.

The *Republic* is the most complicated dialogue considered here at least in virtue of its being the most contradictory. Socrates is often against the doctrines he is most for in other places, and he is much worse against these than when he is for them. The examples of his resentful misanthropy and his almost inconceivable censorship of poetry are only the two most obvious. Yet even in the *Republic* Socrates is complicated and not always as he seems. For example, his excoriation of poetry relies heavily on and alludes to those very Homeric verses he is ostensibly against, so that Socrates' method seems to contradict his message. Even so, in many places, such as his belief in the common over the individual good and his profound understanding of the contradictions inherent in human nature, he is as good here as he is in discussing these matters in other places, with other interlocutors.

The preceding argument takes into account three metaphysical assumptions from which Socrates never diverges. These take the form of binary oppositions which are never disturbed anywhere in the Platonic texts. Socrates believes in the superiority of the soul over the body; of being over becoming; and of reason over the irrational. Throughout the preceding discussion, Socrates struggles to delineate ethical possibilities within these metaphysical constraints. From the dichotomy of soul and body, Socrates discovers and teaches the ethical imperative of living so that bodily appetites do not corrupt the soul's potential for real knowledge. From the dichotomy of being over becoming, Socrates demonstrates how the philosophic life is best suited for allowing human imperfection the possibility of approaching the divine. Socrates is at his most creative when he is concerned with the third dichotomy. Socrates redefines reason to include its opposite, showing both by argument and by the example of his own life that reason is the faculty most necessary to the good human life. Human reason, and the higher order pleasures accompanying it, is what Socrates believes the good human life requires.

These three ethical imperatives can connect Socrates with a tradition which often seems quite hostile to him. Although Nietzsche specifically repudiates Platonic metaphysics and Socrates himself, his own ethical recommendations are compatible with the Socratic ethics identified here. Nietzsche dismisses the metaphysical dichotomies which are the foundation of Socratic ethics, yet the ethics he supports does not similarly refute the Socratic ethical imperatives. Despite their contradictory sources and equally contradictory goals, the ethical views of Socrates and Nietzsche are not in any significant way inconsistent. In the following chapter, the details of this assertion and its significance are developed. Socrates himself is not completely consistent throughout the dialogues, yet for the most part an examination of Plato's work as a whole does yield a systematic view of Socrates' ethical position. In the next chapter, Socrates' ethical position is compared with Nietzsche's. In the third chapter, three otherwise unrelated literary characters are scrutinized with a view to illustrating three different ethical possibilities all of which fall within and can be analyzed according to the Socratic and Nietzschean philosophies of everyday life.

Keeping in mind these many contradictions yet considering the whole, Socrates suggests a way of life that allows the incompleteness of becoming inherent in human existence to approach the perfect being that is the life of the gods. He suggests and attempts to prove the nature of this way of life in his many conversations with so many different interlocutors, and at least as much if not more so through the example of his own life. Much remains to be said of Plato's philosophy itself, even of Plato's philosophy as manifest in the life and death of Socrates. The significance of Socrates' life becomes even more clear when considered along with other, later philosophers and their thoughts, theories, and observations. The history of literature offers many characters who can be much more thoroughly understood by the reader who has attempted to come to terms with and understand Socrates and the Platonic and Socratic influences on Western thought. The thoughts and observations passed over here are of necessity constrained in many ways and dangerously incomplete. They merely serve to indicate important and often overlooked qualities of Socratic thought; and that this thought is not always as it seems. The following chapters will consider other important figures and their relation to Socrates with respect to the idea of philosophy as lived philosophy, and the ongoing developments in philosophy and literature of a workable philosophy of everyday life.

Chapter Two

Nietzsche on Socrates:
The Evasion of Metaphysics
Yields a Practical Ethic

He is utterly alone, time seems nothing to him, he has abandoned hope:thus his universal glance again descends into the depths, and this time to the very bottom:there he sees that suffering pertains to the essence of things and from then on, grown as it were more impersonal, he accepts his own share of suffering more calmly. [65]

The epigram at the start of this chapter refers to Richard Wagner, and comes from Friedrich Nietzsche's early essay "Richard Wagner in Bayreuth," from one of his earliest books, the *Untimely Meditations*. Despite its early origin and specific context, it nevertheless reveals Nietzsche's instinctual reaction to his Nineteenth Century European world. It indicates his awareness of conditions of solitude, hopelessness, and pessimism. Fear followed by acceptance of the depth of suffering; then, suddenly, a hopeful and individual possibility for the transformation of suffering into creativity and joy. This passage demonstrates Nietzsche's faith that Wagner's art and music has revolutionary possibilities for European life, and in his early writings he connects this hope with Greek antiquity and the philosophy of Schopenhauer. Soon Nietzsche will break

---

[65] Nietzsche, Friedrich."Richard Wagner in Bayreuth."*Untimely Meditations*.R. J. Hollingdale, trans. Cambridge University Press:Cambridge, 1995, p. 231.

with many of his early influences. He revises his views on the Greeks, falls out with Wagner, and renounces Schopenhauer. Yet the mood of the above lines and their implications never leaves his writing. The main work under consideration below is *Thus Spoke Zarathustra*. This passage on Wagner from *Untimely Meditations* accurately summarizes Zarathustra's struggle, also. And as his time for writing drew to a close, Nietzsche echoed the same sentiments written here for Wagner, later put into the mouth of Zarathustra, in his own voice in *Ecce Homo*. Throughout this chapter the intimations of this epigram will recur in discussions of Nietzsche's development of specific life philosophies: a profound and influential metaphysics that is at the same time a renunciation of metaphysics; a systematic and coherent philosophy that is at the same time a denouncement of all system-making; and compelling, convincing ethical imperatives that are at the same time uniquely his own, by implication and by definition not to be followed by any but himself.

The previous chapter suggests and limns a group of observations, theories, and interpretations which surface in a consideration of a philosophy of everyday life, particularly those that arise in the philosophy of Socrates as it develops throughout the Platonic dialogues. Plato considered many different perspectives on ideas such as the manner in which an individual lives; the way he comes to terms with his convictions; how best to cultivate his soul; and, the ways in which he goes about his education. It is compelling to see these different theories and perspectives manifest in the character of Socrates. Socrates' lifestyle and the Platonic philosophy he expounds yield practical ethical imperatives illustrative for anyone with an interest in how and why he lives his life. This chapter interprets Nietzsche's metaphysics and ethics within the context of Platonic thought. Much like Plato, Nietzsche exemplifies tenets of his philosophy through a literary figure who appears in his writings; however, unlike Plato's immortalization of his teacher Socrates, Nietzsche is often his own character. In the book most often under consideration below, he voices his developing philosophy through the mouth of his Zarathustra.

What follows is an analysis of the way Nietzsche writes about some of the ideas that Socrates has concluded are important in terms of right-living in day-to-day affairs. These ideas are then considered within the rubric of Nietzsche's overarching and unavoidable intellectual edifices, called periodically throughout what follows "ethical metaphors" because they are linguistic constructions which beget ethical imperatives:the eternal recurrence, the overman, and the will to power. Just as the previous chapter derived Socratic imperatives from metaphysical assumptions, so these Nietzschean philosophic/metaphorical theories lead quite clearly to imperatives for right-living. Also under consideration and important in connection with the ideas at work in Nietzsche's writings is the unique and variegated style of his different books, and the implications deriving from his re-creation of himself as a literary figure. Just as the character of Socrates is instrumental in providing possibilities for understanding Platonic thought, the formidable and often daunting Nietzsche is both writer of new and dangerous philosophies and innocent figure forged by accidents and moved inexorably along by fate.

As in the previous chapter, in what follows the basic assumptions of Nietzsche's metaphysics are seen to yield practical ethical imperatives. Much of Nietzsche's metaphysics seems a mere reversal of the Platonic metaphysics. Nevertheless the ethical imperatives of both Socrates and Nietzsche are remarkably similar and harmonious. In keeping with the spirit of Nietzsche's unsystematic and desultory style of philosophizing, this chapter moves from idea to idea, elaborating them, tying them together, setting them in opposition to Socrates, but not in any particular order other than that which presents itself naturally from a reading of the Platonic and Nietzschean texts. One example of the purpose and style of this chapter is the Socratic and Nietzschean treatments of the dichotomy so crucial to the Western philosophic tradition:the bifurcation of soul and body. This is a fundamental point of departure for the considerations of this chapter, and the purpose of this thesis in expounding a philosophy of everyday life.

Nietzsche elides Socrates' dichotomy of body and soul: for Nietzsche, the soul, if anything, is merely a word about the body, and in his metaphysics primacy is given to the body. Ethically, he connects the primacy of the body with his emphasis on individuality and an idea of order of rank of bodily drives, and with the related concept of the overman. Nietzsche gives primacy to becoming over being, insofar as he does not believe, metaphysically, in anything eternal and unchanging. He connects this metaphysical belief to his idea of the eternal recurrence, from which he derives practical ethical imperatives for the best way to live. Whereas Socrates pitted reason again passion, in ways more complicated than often thought, Nietzsche gives primacy to instinct over his formulation of reason as mere cleverness. The primacy of instinct is related to his notion of the will to power, which clearly yields practical ethical imperatives. All of these facets of Nietzsche's worldview are elaborated below, and connected with real practical imperatives for a philosophy of everyday life. And as demonstrated below, incompatible metaphysical positions do not necessarily preclude a compatible ethical position; in fact, Nietzsche and Socrates are surprisingly similar in their prescriptions for the best possible human life, neverminding what may be their different motivations in so prescribing.

In what follows, the metaphysics and ethics of Socrates and Nietzsche are considered together. Prior to the those considerations however, it is instructive to see exactly what Nietzsche had to say about Socrates, and whether he can be taken at his word in view of the arguments to come. Certainly as early as his *Birth of Tragedy* Nietzsche is already identifying and concerning himself with a danger he perceived in Socrates, connecting Socratic reason with what he calls the Apollonian, in contrast to the Dionysian.[66] Nietzsche fears Socrates started the process of subsuming the latter, which is more instinctual, spontaneous, and life affirming, to the

---

[66] Nietzsche, Friedrich. "The Birth of Tragedy." *Basic Writings of Nietzsche.* Walter Kaufmann, trans. Random House: New York, 1992, pp. 82–83.

former, which is rigid, stifling, worldweary and life-denying. This reading of Socrates and Nietzsche's unfavorable contrasting of the Socratic/Apollonian with the Dionysian persists throughout his writings. Yet in the *Gay Science* Nietzsche seems explicitly to acknowledge his philosophic debt to Socrates, a position he reverses in later works, writing, "I admire the courage and wisdom of Socrates in everything he did, said— and did not say," and referring to Socrates as, "This mocking and enamored monster."[67] And he continues for about a paragraph in the same vein. What Nietzsche refers to as "courage and wisdom" is what has been elaborated in the previous chapter, and includes both Socrates' philosophic way of life and the specific philosophies his way created. Nietzsche owes a great stylistic and philosophic debt, one he often attempts to deny, to this Socratic "courage and wisdom," as he himself calls it. And though Nietzsche's own mocking style is clearly similar to Socratic irony, perhaps Nietzsche, despite protesting the contrary, resented not being equally enamored.

In *Twilight of the Idols* Nietzsche devotes three successive parts to Socrates and Platonic metaphysics, and to what he argues is its ongoing and deleterious influence on the history of Western philosophy. It is not necessary to quote at length from these sections, but pointing to some specific lines is helpful for seeing Nietzsche's harsh and extreme reversal of his public opinion of Socrates. Nietzsche charges Socrates with devaluing the body by equating life with sickness. This is an accusation which is at the bottom of their metaphysical differences, and a large part of what is often considered Nietzsche's reversal of Platonic metaphysics.[68] Nietzsche also makes an implicit contrast between his own belief in ordering the drives of

---

[67] Nietzsche, Friedrich. "The Gay Science." *The Portable Nietzsche.* Walter Kaufmann, trans. Viking Penguin Inc.: New York, 1982, p. 101.

[68] Nietzsche, Friedrich. "Twilight of the Idols." *The Portable Nietzsche.* Walter Kaufmann, trans. Viking Penguin Inc.: New York, 1982, p. 473.

the soul and the Socratic image of a divided soul ordered by reason, charging Socrates with "the admitted wantonness and anarchy of instincts," a charge which, in view of the previous chapter, seems to depend upon an untenable misreading of Plato.[69] And Nietzsche continues in these sections to contrast Platonic metaphysics with his own reversal of that metaphysics, himself suggesting Zarathustra as exemplifying and making manifest this contrast.[70] That Nietzsche's critique is neither as honest nor as easily defensible as his praise is demonstrated by an analysis of the significance of the extent of his metaphysical parting with the Platonic Socrates, and an examination of his ethical congruence with Socrates' philosophy and lifestyle. This is in keeping with Nietzsche's own admonition that "These wisest men of all ages—they should first be scrutinized closely."[71] This thesis is an instance of that scrutiny, and this chapter holds Nietzsche to his own warning.

In considering Socrates and Nietzsche together, the most striking way in which they are in agreement is with respect to creating a philosophy that is connected in a fundamental way to daily human life. Where they differ is with respect to the metaphysics supporting this: whether merely toward the achievement of the good life here in this world, or for the improvement of the chances of a more satisfactory afterlife. Where their ethics converge, their metaphysics contradict; so that despite contrary underlying assumptions, both philosophers arrive often at similar conclusions. Further, despite his many polemics against Socrates, Nietzsche seems often to demonstrate the opposite both in his life and his thought. An instance of this phenomenon, the congruence of their thinking in the face of contradictory assumptions and Nietzsche's unacknowledged approbation of Socrates, can be discerned in a consideration of Nietzsche's well-known and important theory of the eternal recurrence. This theory

---

[69] ibid., 475.

[70] ibid., 486.

[71] ibid., 473.

connects with Socrates' theories of the immortality of the soul in ways curiously overlooked in the secondary literature. Socrates assumes a dichotomy of body and soul, at all times deferring to the importance of the latter over the former. Nietzsche however takes an opposite tack, arguing for the primacy of the body and treating the soul as a metaphor for forces at work within the body.

Just as Socrates returns continuously to the theme of the importance of the soul, to the importance of cultivating a physical life that has as its goal the benefit of the soul, Nietzsche is concerned consistently throughout his various writings with the importance of the human body, of properly reverencing it and with creating a life for oneself which has as its goal the immediate concerns of this earthly world. Nietzsche clearly opposes philosophies that give primacy to otherworldliness, such as to the kingdom of heaven and to the realm of the forms, over the earth and to the soul over the body. His feeling is that there is only one world, this one, and only one body, and that life should reaffirm this world and this body rather than pass over its importance in the anticipation of something supernatural. This belief is an important theme in *Thus Spoke Zarathustra*, and Zarathustra often attempts to teach it to those he encounters during his travels. Concerning his belief in the importance of the earthly world, Zarathustra teaches "No longer to bury one's head in the sand of heavenly things, but to bear it freely, an earthly head, which creates a meaning for the earth."[72] This is an interesting metaphor because burying one's head in the sand illustrates concern for the otherworldly, and holding one's head high refers to thisworldly, earthly concerns. But part of Zarathustra's charm as a literary character is his unique use of language. There is also in this passage an implicit connection to the whole of Nietzsche's thought, which is Zarathustra's observation that the task falls to each individual to create his own meaning for this life. Contrary to Socrates, who believed in

---

[72] Nietzsche, Friedrich. "Thus Spoke Zarathustra." *The Portable Nietzsche*. Walter Kaufmann, trans. Viking Penguin Inc.:New York, 1982, p.144.

one universal meaning that could be attained in varying degrees by different seekers, Nietzsche believes that meaning does not exist other than as it is created in the process of life. Although there is a clear metaphysical contrast between the Socratic belief in eternal and unchanging truths that can be attained in varying degrees and the Nietzschean belief in the individual creation of value, there is also a clear ethical agreement. It is the practice of philosophy that contributes to the ability of the individual to cultivate his soul, for Socrates, and to the creation of individual value in human life, for Nietzsche.

Continuing concerning his belief in the importance of the body Nietzsche's Zarathustra teaches, "But the awakened and knowing say:body am I entirely, and nothing else; and soul is only a word for something about the body."[73] Just like immediately above, here again Zarathustra makes interesting use of language. For both Socrates and Nietzsche the phenomenon of language and the activity of using language to explain ideas is cause for concern. Just as Socrates concerns himself specifically with the nature of language in the dialogue *Philebus*, Nietzsche devotes a very well-known essay, *On Truth and Lie in an Extramoral Sense*, to that same theme. In this particular passage from *Zarathustra* Nietzsche is suggesting that contrary to the common perception, the concept of soul is merely a metaphor for some intangible quality of the body, rather than an entity of its own. This is an important idea because it allows Nietzsche to develop a concept of the soul which not only fails to contradict his belief in the primacy of the body, but goes along with it hand-in-glove. This is his theory of ordering the drives of the soul in such a way as to subject the many weaker, contradictory drives and inclinations to the greatest and most important one. It is an idea he concerns himself with quite often and in many different places, and which is clearly compatible with Socrates' prescriptions for right-living. For Nietzsche the soul is a metaphor allowing for a greater understanding

---

[73] ibid., 146.

of the heretofore underappreciated importance of the human body. This metaphor and its metaphysical presuppositions lead to his practical recommendations for the self-mastery of contradictory internal motivations. For Socrates, the soul is the divine and fragile component of the body which philosophy preserves in spite of the many and manifold dangers it encounters during its embodiment in human life. Nietzsche's concern, often leveled explicitly against Plato, such as in *Twilight of the Idols*, is that the Platonic/Socratic metaphysics of the soul has led to a dangerous devaluing of human life. Yet clearly this is not through any fault of Socrates', whose ethical way of life clearly anticipates and satisfies the conditions of Nietzsche's ethics.

Through Zarathustra and elsewhere Nietzsche teaches that if there is a soul, it is only important insofar as it is a component of and subsumed beneath the body. The living should concern themselves with their bodies as if that were all they have; and if they are concerned with their souls, it is only through their bodies that they can affect it. Zarathustra redefines Socratic virtue, teaching that virtuous living is living for the earth:"Alas, there has always been so much virtue that has flown away. Lead back to the earth the virtue that flew away, as I do—back to the body, back to life, that it may give the earth a meaning, a human meaning."[74] Once again is the notion that virtue belongs to the earth, despite the fact that in the past it has spurned the earth out of misguided concern for the beyond; that is, that virtue involves the creation of meaning for human life. This ongoing concern is related to Nietzsche's theory of the slave revolt in morality, some implications of which are discussed below, which has caused near-universal acceptance of the belief that virtue is by definition and inherently otherworldly. Nietzsche's genealogy of the slave revolt in morality and his analysis of its implications reads easily as a history of the misapplication, even misinterpretation of Socratic philosophy over the course of

---

[74] ibid., 188.

the Western philosophical tradition. Perhaps this misinterpretation begins as early the time of Socrates himself, originating in the trial Plato relates in his *Apology*, and continuing through Nietzsche's *Genealogy of Morals*.

Zarathustra teaches that virtue is for this life, this body; concern for giving a human meaning to the earth. It is only the weak, those behind the slave revolt in morality, for whom virtue is otherworldly:"For all these have an unclean spirit—but especially those who have neither rest nor repose except when they see the world from *abaft*, the afterworldly."75 Zarathustra reproaches those whose only earthly concern is the after-worldly with the appellation "unclean of spirit," in an ironic reversal, rem-iniscent of Socrates, of what is more commonly considered to dull the spirit and what to elevate it. It is Nietzsche's theory of the slave revolt in morality which explains how it came to be that so much virtue has, as Zarathustra says, flown away; whereas it is his theories of the eternal recur-rence, love of fate, the overman, and other related ideas which identify the practical possibility of overcoming this inauthentic though widespread way of life.

It is not only Nietzsche's Zarathustra who is consistently of this opin-ion, Nietzsche advocates it quite adamantly in his autobiographical *Ecce Homo*. Near the very end of this work he forcefully proclaims that,

> The concept of the "beyond," the "true world" invented in order to devaluate the only world there is—in order to retain no goal, no reason, no task for our earthly reality! The concept of the "soul," the "spirit," finally even "*immortal* soul," invented in order to despise the body, to make it sick, "holy"; to oppose with a ghastly levity everything that deserves to be taken seriously in life, the questions of nourishment, abode, spiritual diet, treat-ment of the sick, cleanliness, and weather.76

---

75 ibid., 316.

76 Nietzsche, Friedrich."Ecce Homo." *Basic Writings of Nietzsche*.Walter Kaufmann, trans.Random House:New York, 1992, p. 790.

In this passage Nietzsche reiterates even more explicitly the teachings of his Zarathustra on the importance of the earthly world and body. He goes so far as to say not only that belief in the afterworld devalues this world, but that the afterworld was in fact invented for that purpose. This idea, which can easily be read as an accusation of Plato and Socrates, is the premise of Nietzsche's genealogies. Nietzsche is concerned with the fact that the phenomenon described in this passage leads to taking what is most serious in life least seriously: physical and spiritual diet, dwelling place, and physical health. He wants to shift philosophy's concern from spiritual to bodily matters, and retain an interest in spiritual matters only insofar as they are another way of looking at the body and its earthly world. These thoughts occupied Nietzsche not only as late as the writing of *Ecce Homo*, as seen here, but as early as *Human, All-Too-Human*, in which place he writes that "*Everything* else must be of more concern to us than that which has hitherto been preached to us as the most important of all things—I mean the questions:what is the purpose of man? What is his fate after death? How can he be reconciled with God?—and all the rest of these *curiosa*."[77] Here as elsewhere Nietzsche is explicit on the matter of the primacy of the world of immediacy, this world, this life over any more traditionally or more commonly believed theory that this world and its life is merely a preparation for the afterlife. Nietzsche advocates a complete reversal of what his been considered worthy of thought by the tradition. These passages help to demonstrate Nietzsche's vehement and consistent opposition to Platonic metaphysics. And yet when read along with Socratic philosophy, they seem more to indicate the ongoing misunderstanding of Socrates than dangers truly inherent in the Socratic way of life.

Nietzsche and Socrates' perspectives on one of philosophy's most ancient topics, the dichotomy of the body and the soul, is useful in considering

---

[77] Nietzsche, Friedrich. *Human All-Too-Human:A Book for Free Spirits*.R. J. Hollingdale, trans.Cambridge University Press:New York, 1994, volume 2, part 2, 16. (citation given of aphorism number).

their shared emphasis on lived philosophy because of the many ways in which their views on this dichotomy inform their other theories and beliefs. Socrates' belief in the dichotomy of the body and the soul informs his ideas on education, immortality, virtue, and right-living. It is a primary assumption which subtends many if not all of his other assertions. Throughout Nietzsche's writings a parallel but contrary belief obtains, informing many of his theories, ideas, observations, and other of his beliefs. As argued above, for Nietzsche it is a belief in the primacy of the body over and even to the exclusion of the soul which is fundamental. Included among the many theories of his with which this belief connects is the idea of the eternal recurrence. Although this may not be immediately clear, an examination of the texts demonstrates the necessary connection inherent in the conception of the primacy of the body and the notion of the eternal recurrence, both to one another and to the substance of a Nietzschean philosophy of everyday life.

An example of Nietzsche's general idea of the eternal recurrence is found in *Thus Spoke Zarathustra*. In a conversation between Zarathustra and the spirit of gravity Zarathustra explains the eternal recurrence with a particularly striking metaphor. Zarathustra suggests that he and his archenemy, the spirit of gravity, are standing before a gate called "moment." A long road stretches behind them, continuing through the gate and on beyond. Both behind and in front of them the road stretches on infinitely. After setting up this image Zarathustra asks his archenemy, "Must not whatever *can* happen have happened, have been done, have passed by before," leading him to ask the question, "Must we not eternally return?"[78] In this formulation of the eternal recurrence Nietzsche is suggesting that everything happening in the world has already happened an infinite number of times in the past, and will happen again an infinite number of times. Built into Zarathustra's concept of infinity is the fact that in an infinite period of time, by definition every possible event will

---

[78] *Zarathustra*, 270.

have occurred, and will have repeated itself time and again, infinitely. Similarly, every possible event is continuing to recur into the future, an infinite number of times. This is what Nietzsche is describing through this image.

For Zarathustra this is at first a source of concern because he is unhappy with the condition of man and the eternal recurrence suggests that he will always be unhappy because man will always be the same as he is now. Zarathustra exclaims, "Alas, man recurs eternally! The small man recurs eternally!"[79] In this particular formulation the eternal recurrence is set up as a function of the world itself, rather than a comportment within the world by the individuals peopling it. This is an inherently disappointing and disempowering definition of the eternal recurrence, and it is not surprising that Zarathustra is discouraged and pessimistic. But only until he realizes his love for life and his belief in the possibility for individual overcoming, which allows his nausea to transform into joy. This realization begins in the conclusion of the very section just quoted, in which he describes this first formulation of the eternal recurrence. Zarathustra's realization progresses throughout the text in more certain and thorough formulations, and in connection with early developments of the concepts of the overman and the will to power. Nietzsche also returns to the significance of this realization about the nature of the eternal recurrence in his more mature formulations of that theory in other texts.

Much like Socrates in so many places ironically attributes his speeches to other sources, in *Zarathustra* Nietzsche is able to mask himself behind a fictional literary character. However, in his other books he employs no such critical distance, and in *Ecce Homo* at least he is explicitly autobiographical. The ideas expressed by Zarathustra Nietzsche expresses in his own voice in numerous places. In *Beyond Good and Evil* Nietzsche talks about "The ideal of the most high-spirited, alive, and world-affirming

---

[79] ibid., 331.

human being who has not only come to terms and learned to get along with whatever was and is, but who wants to have *what was and is* repeated into all eternity".[80] Here is his revision of the earlier formulation of the eternal recurrence, though the distinction between the two is primarily implicit and requires some explanation in order to become clear. Unlike Zarathustra's formulation, here the eternal recurrence is not so much a quality of the world as it is a way for the individual to live in the world. If one has overcome oneself in the highest possible degree then one is in a position to will that if the world could recur again, it should be exactly how it was the first time around. This may not be a real possibility, but as a personal outlook it represents the most an individual could possibly accomplish. What Nietzsche is describing is the conjunction in practice of his several most fundamental theories:the eternal recurrence, love of fate, willfulness, and the acceptance of the primacy of the earth. This interpretation is connected with, and even brought to mind through the language of the above-quoted passage, another of Nietzsche's theories considered below in connection with Socrates, the idea of the overman. Realizing possibilities for self-overcoming creates the possibility of the overman, insofar as that is understood as a human possibility as opposed to something historical or external.

In his later writings Nietzsche remains concerned with these issues. For example, in talking about "the eternal joy of becoming" in *Twilight of the Idols* Nietzsche writes, "Saying Yes to life even in its strangest and hardest problems, the will to life rejoicing over its own inexhaustibility even in the very sacrifice of its highest types—*that* is what I called Dionysian, *that* is what I guessed to be the bridge to the psychology of the *tragic* poet".[81]In this passage he quite explicitly supports the interpretation of the eternal recurrence as an approach toward life for which one can strive. Nietzsche

---

[80] Nietzsche, Friedrich."Beyond Good and Evil." *Basic Writings of Nietzsche.*Walter Kaufmann, trans.Random House:New York, 1992, p. 258.

[81] *TI*, 562.

connects this striving to some sort of creative output, and to his ideas of the Dionysian and the will to power. But unlike his much earlier position in which he connects creativity to Wagnerian opera, here there is the indication that the ultimate creative act manifests itself in the individual human life. Zarathustra creates his life out of his philosophy, and Nietzsche does the same. Any Nietzschean imperative for right-living cannot remain only within the bounds of theory. His imperatives, culled from his various ethical metaphors, are powerful because they are lived, not merely thought. The Socratic and Nietzschean ethical imperatives originate in lived philosophies.

Implicit in Nietzsche's discussions of the primacy of becoming and the eternal recurrence is a connection between those two ideas. The former is a potentially dangerous assertion insofar as it removes a long-standing foundation for human action, the existence of eternal and unchanging truths. The latter becomes a recommendation, even an imperative, which is able to rescue individual human possibilities from plummeting into nothingness from lack of an eternal and unchanging foundation. Nietzsche continues to deal with this topic in his last book. In *Ecce Homo* Nietzsche explains just how the particular above-cited passage from *Twilight of the Idols* connects to the eternal recurrence:

> The affirmation of passing away *and destroying*, which is the decisive feature of a Dionysian philosophy; saying Yes to opposition and war; *becoming*, along with a radical repudiation of the very concept of *being*—all this is clearly more closely related to me than anything else thought to date. The doctrine of the "eternal recurrence," that is, of the unconditional and infinitely repeated circular course of all things—this doctrine of Zarathustra *might* in the end have been taught already by Heraclitus.[82]

---

82 *EH*, 729.

This passage is important for a number of reasons. In the first four lines Nietzsche, like Heraclitus in opposition to Parmenides, stresses the importance of a worldview in which something must be destroyed in order for something new to be built, often, as he says elsewhere, from the remains of what has been destroyed. This is his emphasis on creativity as virtue, and its connection to his contra-Platonic metaphysics of becoming. Life is a continual progression of one thing overtaking and changing another, only to be overtaken itself; hence the emphasis of becoming, or changing and moving on, over being, or static diachronic enduring. He considers this view the closest thing to him, and in the next few lines calls this view the doctrine of the eternal recurrence and likens it to Heraclitus' philosophy. What makes the interpretation of the eternal recurrence as a way of life rather than a scientific law especially convincing is that it is hinted at in earlier works as well as elaborated on and expounded in these later books.

Of primary importance here in terms of connecting Nietzsche and Socrates on the point of a philosophy of everyday life and of the purpose of philosophy as a lived philosophy, is that in the passage just cited Nietzsche completely contradicts Socrates' main assertion. Nietzsche disputes the primacy of being over becoming and asserts entirely the opposite; but, for the same purpose. The determination of the best way to come to terms with the exigencies of everyday life. So that inherently contradictory metaphysical assumptions of Socrates and Nietzsche nevertheless allow them to derive importantly similar ethical conclusions, leading them to equally similar practical ethical imperatives for daily human life. In the *Phaedo* Socrates proves the immortality of the soul, and it is from this immortality, proven in the *Phaedo* and assumed in so many other places, that Socrates derives his assertion that philosophy provides the best possible way of life. For Socrates, there is a direct connection between the primacy of the soul and the importance of philosophy. As demonstrated here, Nietzsche asserts and defends a metaphysics giving primacy to the body, and there is a clear and direct connection between the primacy of the body and the eternal recurrence. It is in this way, from a contradictory metaphysics, that Nietzsche arrives at conclusions so similar to Socrates', regarding a way of life most conducive to accepting and affirming the eternal recurrence; what amounts to an introspective, philosophic way of life.

As alluded to above, Nietzsche's theory of the eternal recurrence is conceptually connected with his equally ubiquitous notion of the overman. The idea of the overman and the qualities inherent in him by definition cannot help but call the readers attention to Socrates, both in terms of the way Socrates conducted his own affairs, up to and including his death, and his more general pronouncements on the best way to live the good life. This idea and these qualities include the process of self-overcoming, a certain fatalism, and even willfulness in the face of that fatalism, and coming to terms with issues such as resentment and morality. Socrates, often accused by Nietzsche as the first of the "Last Men" (*Twilight of the Idols*, *Gay Science*), would seem rather to be solidly among the "philosophers of the future," whose creativity and joy anticipate the future possibility of Nietzsche's overman (*Beyond Good and Evil, Genealogy of Morals*).

The overman, Nietzsche writes in *Genealogy of Morals*, the "man of the future," is "The *redeeming* man of great love and contempt, the creative spirit whose compelling strength will not let him rest in any aloofness or any beyond, whose isolation is misunderstood by the people as if it were flight *from* reality."[83] In this late passage Nietzsche brings together many qualities of the overman:the overman's creativity and strength; his eschewing of a belief in an afterworld; and, perhaps most intriguingly, his misunderstood solitude. This passage also recalls the figure of Socrates to the reader, reminding one of the *Apology*, for example, and the many other instances of Socrates' being misunderstood by his contemporaries. The most obvious difference between Socrates and Nietzsche with respect to

---

83 Nietzsche, Friedrich."Genealogy of Morals." *Basic Writings of Nietzsche.*Walter Kaufmann, trans.Random House:New York, 1992, p. 532.

this passage is once again clearly metaphysical:that Socrates will in fact rest in the "beyond;" and yet the ethical similarities are more striking. Both are misunderstood, and both are looking to philosophy to provide necessary perspective to life in general and to their everyday lives in particular. In this passage redemption is clearly asserted to be a possibility for this world, or not at all. The traditional association handed down to Western thinking by Plato of reality with what is after or above rather than what is here is resisted. Nietzsche rescues spirit from the old concept of reality and reassigns it to his new concept of reality, reality as what is physical and earthly, and connects it with creativity and the strength that creativity requires. And this passage is not unique; its insights echo and resound throughout Nietzschean thought.

But what must be considered in an examination of Nietzsche's philosophy, and in connection with what has already been said above, is the relationship of the overman to the eternal recurrence. What the text points to is an understanding of the overman not as a single man who will come to the world at some later time and redeem it; but rather as seems to be indicated by this passage,as a possibility that man can achieve if he is able to believe in, or will, the eternal recurrence. The overman is not a savior, but a transformation of man through his own self-overcoming. There is much evidence supporting this interpretation throughout all of Nietzsche's texts. Early in *Human, All-Too-Human* he writes, "One should speak only when one may not stay silent; and then only of that which one has *overcome*— everything else is chatter, 'literature', lack of breeding."[84] Nietzsche wants to regard his writings as being about his own process of self-overcoming; it is this which truly occupies his thought and necessitates all of his philosophizing. This is why he is so often referring to finding his own style

---

[84] *HH*, volume 2, preface, 1.

and his own way, and why this theme is related to all of the others in his works.[85]

Once again this analysis of Nietzsche lends itself to a comparison with Socrates. Nietzsche specifically considers his writings a record of his own process of self-overcoming. This is an inherently individualistic process. His experiences and the writings they engendered may, as argued here, yield useful practical imperatives for others, but that is not to say they pave pathways, which they do not. Socrates is of a much different opinion than this for at least two reasons; and though these may not both be strictly metaphysical, yet they are differences which do not preclude their both arriving at similar self-opinions, and similar ethical imperatives. First, Nietzsche's assessment of his own practice of writing is analogous to Socrates' resistance to writing anything down. Socrates believes philosophy is a way of life. He conducts himself in accordance with his philosophy, conversing with whoever may come along, demonstrating his ideas and his reasoning to whoever wishes to attach himself to him as a pupil. The whole of the Platonic dialogues is an illustration of this. But unlike Nietzsche, Socrates believes he is following a path that the gods have pointed out to him, and that others, if so inclined, can follow with him. He believes that he can lead his interlocutors, through a process of

---

[85] For example, through the mouth of Zarathustra Nietzsche explains that, "'This is my way; where is yours?'—thus I answered those who asked me 'the way.' For *the* way—that does not exist." *Zarathustra*, 307. Also much earlier Nietzsche makes abundantly clear his emphasis on the importance of cultivating one's own individuality: "We are responsible to ourselves for our own existence; consequently we want to be the true helmsman of this existence and refuse to allow our existence to resemble a mindless act of chance," "No one can construct for you the bridge upon which precisely you must cross the stream of life, no one but you yourself alone," "There exists in the world a single path along which no one can go except you: whither does it lead? Do not ask, go along it." Nietzsche, Friedrich. "Schopenhauer as Educator." *Untimely Meditations*. R. J. Hollingdale, trans. Cambridge University Press: Cambridge 1995, pp. 128, 129. This theme is also implicit throughout *Ecce Homo*.

questioning, to the same conclusions he has reached. That they in turn could do the same for others is evidenced by Plato's influence on philosophy, including, as implicit throughout this thesis, on Nietzsche. Second, both agree that philosophy is a way of life, not merely a way of thinking, though it may include that. Philosophy is a vocation more than a profession. It is the idea that philosophy is lived and not merely thought that is shared by both Nietzsche and Socrates. The difference between them, that for Socrates it is a preparation for death but for Nietzsche a way to give meaning to life, seems not as important after this type of analysis than it may seem at first glance.

The theme of self-overcoming informing the preceding discussion is one that occupies Nietzsche in much of *Zarathustra*. In the first of the four parts of that book, Zarathustra speaks to the people in the marketplace of a town, saying "*I teach you the overman*. Man is something that shall be overcome. What have you done to overcome him?"[86] Both this question itself and the narrative frame surrounding it serve to indicate that Nietzsche's overman is not a real person, but a possibility for self-overcoming. Zarathustra's nausea at mankind and his fear of the eternal recurrence result from the fact that no one he meets has even taken a step towards that end. This interpretation of the overman is supported even further by the following often quoted metaphor of Zarathustra's: "Man is a rope, tied between beast and overman—a rope over an abyss. A dangerous across, a dangerous on-the-way, a dangerous looking-back, a dangerous shuddering and stopping."[87] This passage is significant for at least two reasons. First, man is viewed as containing within himself both beast and overman. Each individual must make his own treacherous journey over the abyss of life's potential wretchedness in order to overcome and redeem himself. With his self-overcoming he will recreate himself as the overman and feel joy at his belief in the eternal recurrence. Second, the process of

---

[86] *Zarathustra*, 122.
[87] ibid., 126.

self-overcoming contains within it both a looking-back and an anticipating forward. The self-overcoming individual must be concerned with his past and avoid submitting to a kind of naive determinism with regard to it. He must see how his past made him who he his, the person he is coming to rejoice at being, and must therefore affirm and reaffirm it. That is, he must come to terms with his past in such a way that he begins to will it retroactively. In this way he can move on from his past to his future in such a way that he is willing it and creating and recreating it, rather than merely letting it happen. These passages illustrate the conceptual union of the eternal recurrence and the overman.

That the overman is not a godlike man but rather man finally attaining new perspective over his life is explicitly held forth in the second part of *Zarathustra*. Zarathustra teaches, "Once one said God when one looked upon distant seas; but now I have taught you to say: overman," and he continues, "God is a conjecture; but I desire that your conjectures should not reach beyond your creative will. Could you *create* a god? Then do not speak to me of any gods. But you could well create the overman."[88] Contrary to a common perception, the overman is not anything superhuman, but a man whose creativity and whose strong will allow him to recreate himself as the overman; or, as Zarathustra puts it, "God died: now *we* want the overman to live."[89] Zarathustra believes that it is God who has been giving the world meaning, imparting meaning to the world from His divine heights. He believes it has been anticipation of the world to come, the heavenly afterlife, that has so far given meaning to individual earthly lives. Zarathustra is struggling to give meaning to earth and life in a world where the assumption of the divine is no longer a certainty, and in such a way that the meaning will adhere even if there is no God.

What is discussed in this chapter, philosophy as a way of life which creates meaning for life, is both Zarathustra and Nietzsche's answer to this

---

[88] ibid., 197.
[89] ibid., 399.

most important of questions. Zarathustra's answers, taken up and expounded by Nietzsche in his own voice, are the ethical imperatives argued here, derived from ethical metaphors of eternal recurrence, will to power, and the overman. And it is not only the middle period work *Zarathustra* in which Nietzsche supports this reading. In the *Genealogy of Morals* he quotes at length a passage on this matter originally published in *The Gay Science*:

> To view nature as if it were a proof of the goodness and provi-
> dence of a God; to interpret history to the glory of a divine rea-
> son, as the perpetual witness to a moral world order and moral
> intentions; to interpret one's own experiences, as pious men long
> interpreted them, as if everything were preordained, everything a
> sign, everything sent for the salvation of the soul—that now
> belongs to the *past*, that has the conscience *against* it, that seems
> to every more sensitive conscience indecent, dishonest, menda-
> cious, feminism, weakness, cowardice:it is this rigor if anything
> that makes us *good Europeans* and the heirs of Europe's longest
> and bravest self-overcoming.[90]

This passage is significant with respect to the relationship between self-overcoming and the role of fate in the doctrines of the eternal recurrence and the overman, as discussed immediately below, but it also indicates Nietzsche's continuing support for the interpretation of the overman maintained above. Nietzsche, then, quite clearly writes about the overman as a creation of man out of himself and as the result of his self-overcoming, not as a godlike figure descending from above. It is because of this that the overman's possibility does not contradict the doctrine of the eternal recur-rence, but, quite definitely, each requires and is interrelated with the other.

Nietzsche's overman and his eternal recurrence cannot be understood apart from one another, or apart from Nietzsche's beliefs about fate. His

---

[90] *GM*, 596–597.

discussion of fate spans the whole of his life's work, and his beliefs about fate inform his vehement and incessant attacks on resentment, cleverness, and free will. Nietzsche's most general statement on his feeling towards fate is in *Human, All-Too-Human* where he writes that, "You *have* to believe in fate—science can compel you to. What then grows out of this belief in your case—cowardice, resignation or frankness and magnanimity—bears witness to the soil upon which that seedcorn has been scattered but not, however, to the seedcorn itself—for out of this anything and everything can grow."[91] Nietzsche believes that although everyone is subject to fate, what is important is how each individual comports himself within his fate; whether he overcomes it to achieve a positive and life-affirming worldview, or whether it prompts in him feelings of resignation and resentment. Nietzsche reasserts this belief in *Beyond Good and Evil*, writing "But at the bottom of us, really 'deep down,' there is, of course, something unteachable, some granite of spiritual *fatum*, of predetermined decision and answer to predetermined selected questions."[92] This too is an important passage because it illustrates that for Nietzsche the power an individual has over his life is not his ability to act otherwise than propelled by his circumstances, but rather his ability to bring his will in alignment with his life. These passages indicate that the individual at his most fundamental is nothing other than one small part of an infinite complex, so that at the most basic level he is subject to fate, not, as many would have it, free.

That man cannot be divorced from fate is asserted even more explicitly in *Twilight of the Idols*, where Nietzsche writes that "The single human being is a piece of *fatum* from the front and from the rear, one law more, one necessity more for all that is yet to come and to be."[93] Once again is an illustration of the individual's powerlessness with respect to fate. The

---

[91] *HH*, volume 2, part 1, 363.
[92] *BGE*, 352.
[93] *TI*, 491.

universal interconnectedness Nietzsche observes leads him to suggest that each individual is determined by all who have come before him, and further contributes to the determination of all who will follow. This may a small and subtle, even an indiscernible, influence, but the aggregate of all human population and history makes it significant. This passage and the passage from *Beyond Good and Evil* just quoted, together serve to demonstrate that Nietzsche believes in fate, and believes that it is a basic and unavoidable aspect of the human being. Thus what the self-overcoming individual must be concerned with is not the existence or nonexistence of fate, but how he can come to terms with himself even in spite of his circumstances. So that Nietzsche writes, "Such a spirit who has *become free* stands amid the cosmos with a joyous and trusting fatalism, in the *faith* that only the particular is loathsome, and that all is redeemed and affirmed in the whole—*he does not negate any more.* Such a faith, however, is the highest of all possible faiths:I have baptized it with the name of *Dionysus.*"[94] Notice Nietzsche's Platonic loathing of the particular. Then, a positive relationship to fatalism is necessarily coterminal with self-overcoming. Creativity and self-overcoming are necessarily intertwined, as Zarathustra realizes when he makes his well-known proclamation that "The time is gone when mere accidents could still happen to me; and what could still come to me now that was not mine already? What returns, what finally comes home to me, is my own self and what of myself has long been in strange lands and scattered among all things and accidents."[95] Nothing that happens to Zarathustra is an accident, because even if it were fated for him, if he has reached the degree of self-overcoming where he can will everything that has happened and feel joy rather than nausea at the eternal recurrence, then what has happened to him is for all practical purposes not a result of fate but a result of his own

---

[94] ibid., 554.
[95] *Zarathustra*, 264.

will. This is a clear example of the greater importance of ethics over and against metaphysics for Nietzsche.

In the *Twilight of the Idols* passages mentioned, Nietzsche is discussing this same phenomenon, but in such a way as to apply to human life in general, whereas in *Zarathustra* it is Zarathustra's own style of self-overcoming that Nietzsche is discussing. And looking back on his own life in his last book, Nietzsche continues to support this same position. This is what Nietzsche means when he writes that "Accepting oneself as if fated, not wishing oneself 'different'—that is in such cases *great reason* itself," "I do not want in the least that anything should become different than it is; I myself do not want to become different," and, in perhaps his most famous remark on this matter, "My formula for greatness in a human being is *amor fati*: that one wants nothing to be different, not forward, not backward, not in all eternity."[96] For Nietzsche's Zarathustra, Nietzsche himself, and indeed every single individual who strives to overcome himself, a love of fate does not preclude self-overcoming, rather each proceeds from and engenders the other. Interestingly enough, this is a rather democratic reading of the Nietzschean imperatives, contrary both to the elitist view often attributed to him, and to the elitism of the Socrates of Plato's *Republic*. This indicates that Nietzsche is concerned with ethical possibilities for all individuals rather than with the construction of a metaphysical account of the way the world is.

With a consideration of these broad themes in mind, it is possible to see how Nietzsche's many other, less primary perhaps but equally ubiquitous ideas come to have importance in his overarching philosophy of everyday life, and how they too connect with the practical Socratic worldview. Concerning the idea of *ressentiment*, for example, it is only possible fully to understand Nietzsche's vehemence against resentment in light of the above discussion of his belief in fate. It is the achievement of *amor fati* that would allow an individual to believe with Zarathustra, "But if you

---

[96] *EH*, 687, 711, and 714.

have an enemy, do not requite him evil with good, for that would put him to shame. Rather prove that he did you some good."[97] To prove to someone who believes he has done you evil that he has in fact done you some good is to have that relationship to fate in which you are able to will everything that has happened to you. Truly to believe that you have derived benefit from his evil, that it is good for you, is to realize that the self you have come to will is dependent upon these experiences. This is so important to Zarathustra that he says, "For *that man be delivered from all revenge*, that is for me the bridge to the highest hope, and a rainbow after long storms."[98] The realization of the rainbow is dependent upon the evils of the storms; deliverance from revenge is the bridge between beast and overman. Note the similarity to the image of the tightrope walker. Clearly this is a theme Zarathustra is struggling to develop, especially considering how Part Two of *Zarathustra* closes with his internal struggle with the idea of the eternal recurrence and the ideas connected with it, and his inability to communicate his fearful thoughts to his disciples. Then Part Three opens with Zarathustra's beginning to realize the hopefulness inherent in what he has previously believed is the hopelessness of his thought of the eternal recurrence, as evidenced in his parable of the man with the snake in his mouth which immediately follows in the same section as the parable of the spirit of gravity and the moment in eternity.[99] The development of this theme is not left to Zarathustra alone; Nietzsche takes it up and revises it in his later works, reiterating the hopeful and individualistic aspects, especially, for example, in *Beyond Good and Evil* and *The Genealogy of Morals*. Further, it is instructive to see this transformation in Zarathustra's teaching anticipated already in some of Nietzsche's earliest published writings, such as the epigram at the outset of this chapter.

---

[97] *Zarathustra*, 180.

[98] ibid., 211.

[99] ibid., 270–272.

In one particularly useful passage from the *Genealogy of Morals* which brings together many of these themes, Nietzsche connects this belief about fate and resentment to his famous bifurcation of morality into slave and master moralities. He explains that:

> The slave revolt in morality begins when *ressentiment* itself becomes creative and gives birth to values:the *ressentiment* of natures that are denied the true reaction, that of deeds, and compensate themselves with an imaginary revenge. While every noble morality develops from a triumphant affirmation of itself, slave morality from the outset says No to what is "outside," what is "different," what is "not itself"; and this No is its creative deed.[100]

For Nietzsche, as evidenced in this passage and others, when an individual resents another it is because he is weak and his only means of asserting himself is revenge. Rather than show how his enemy did him some good, the weak and resentful individual wants to take revenge on his enemy. Nietzsche elaborates this theory in social and historical terms, but what is pertinent here is its individual applications within a philosophy of everyday life. Though Nietzsche is speaking generally here, one specific instance of this phenomenon is Socrates' trial. This passage can clearly be seen to describe the feelings and actions of Socrates' accusers. In general, as Nietzsche writes above, and on the contrary, the noble man, acting from a position of strength, is powerful enough not to feel resentment. Just as Socrates, in the *Phaedo* and the *Crito*, does not blame his accusers for his death, or try to avoid his fate through escape and exile, rather accepting his fate and willing it to be as it is. The type of man, and perhaps Socrates is one example, who is able to overcome resentment is one who has reached the point of loving fate and willing all that has happened in his life, which is how resentment and *amor fati* are related.

---

[100] *GM*, 472.

Several of the connections among the many facets of Nietzsche's philosophy of everyday life have been considered, including the relations among the eternal recurrence, self-overcoming, and the concept of the overman. But there are other interesting aspects of his thought which are also connected with these themes. Nietzsche's *amor fati* and his campaign against resentment, for example, are also related to his belief in the importance of instinct in the individual and his disbelief in free will, as the following passage from *Ecce Homo* indicates:

> Born of weakness, *ressentiment* is most harmful for the weak themselves. Conversely, given a rich nature, it is a *superfluous* feeling; mastering this feeling is virtually what proves riches. Whoever knows how seriously my philosophy has pursued the fight against vengefulness and rancor, even in the doctrine of "free will"—the fight against Christianity is merely a special case of this—will understand why I am making such a point of my own behavior, my *instinctive sureness* in practice.[101]

In this passage Nietzsche maintains that resentment is a quality of the weak, who would overcome it if they were to become strong. Nietzsche's disavowal of resentment and free will, and his emphasis on cultivating one's own instinct, is connected with his belief that in order to overcome oneself one must learn to love, reaffirm, and will whatever has been one's fate. Further, this passage is noteworthy with respect to Nietzsche's commitment to a philosophy of everyday life because there is first his underlying assumptions, such as his belief in the importance of instinct, and logical derivations from these assumptions, such as overcoming resentment. This type of interpretation helps to indicate how ethical imperatives are embedded in his thought. Resentment is born of weakness, as seen in his genealogy of the slave revolt in morality, yet is most harmful for the weak, because unable to see beyond it they are the most oppressed by it.

---

[101] *EH*, 687.

The fight against vengefulness is tantamount to revising the concept of free will, transforming it into love of fate and everything entailed by that idea.

Returning to the discussion of Nietzsche's metaphysics, and the ethics it suggests, both implicitly and explicitly, it is instructive to consider how Nietzsche attacks belief in free will in a way similar to his attack on cleverness in favor of instinct, insofar as both of these ideas derive from his *amor fati*. He devotes a large number of aphorisms in *Human All-Too-Human* to disputing the possibility of free will, often calling his belief "the theory of total unaccountability."[102] In one passage near the end of that book he writes how "In reality, however, all our doing and knowing is not a succession of facts and empty spaces but a continuous flux. Now, belief in freedom of will is incompatible precisely with the idea of a continuous, homogenous, undivided, indivisible flowing: it presupposes that *every individual action is isolate and indivisible*; it is an *atomism* in the domain of willing and knowing."[103] This passage, and many others which deal with this idea, explains an observation of Nietzsche's which anticipates the most current theories of contemporary physics: the interconnection of every element of the universe, so that seemingly small causes yield enormous effects in unanticipated ways, and seemingly isolated effects have an infinity of indiscernible causes. This is a radical revision of the entire concept of cause and effect. So that for Nietzsche, the reason free will is impossible is because it presupposes that each individual life is an entity unto itself, and thus can do as it pleases regardless of what any other entity is doing. For Nietzsche, however, each moment in a life is related to every other moment, and each life to every other life. An individual cannot be free because his existence is interwoven with an infinity of other existing beings.

---

102 *HH*, volume 1, part 1, 105.
103 *HH*, volume 2, part 2, 11.

This is why Nietzsche can write that "No one is accountable for his deeds, no one for his nature; to judge is the same thing as to be unjust. This also applies when the individual judges himself."[104] His belief about the relationship that exists among all beings leads him to his theory of total unaccountability, which in turn leads to his opposition to free will. Because man is not free he cannot judge others or himself, which is why Nietzsche argues so strongly against resentment; no human being is justified, according to Nietzsche's thought, in resenting another. However, in *Beyond Good and Evil* Nietzsche explains how unfreedom of the will is as unjustifiable as freedom of the will. He maintains that the attempt to establish a doctrine of free will results from "The desire to bear the entire and ultimate responsibility for one's actions oneself, and to absolve God, the world, ancestors, chance, and society...."[105] Nietzsche finds fault with this desire because it does a disservice to the complexity, ubiquity, and insuperability of influences on human life. There is a subtle difference between this and what would appear to be his mutually exclusive doctrine of *amor fati* which is that the former, disputed approach to accepting one's situation requires a naiveté about these complexities. However, accepting one's life from a position of love of fate involves understating this situation and overcoming it. This subtlety is implicit in the whole of this discussion, and often Nietzsche states it explicitly, such as his imperative to change every "thus it was" into "thus I willed it," in *Zarathustra* and *Ecce Homo*.[106] Continuing in this vein, Nietzsche later writes that, "The 'unfree will' is mythology; in real life it is only a matter of *strong* and *weak* wills."[107] So that although Nietzsche does not believe in free will, that does not mean

---

[104] *HH*, volume 1, part 1, 39.

[105] *BGE*, 218.

[106] "To redeem what is past in man and to re-create all 'it was' until the will says, 'thus I willed it! Thus I shall will it'—this I called redemption and this alone I taught them to call redemption" *Zarathustra*, 310.

[107] *BGE.*, 219.

that he must instead believe in some concept of unfreedom of the will. Just as his belief in fate does not preclude an individual's exercising his own will in his own life. Rather, Nietzsche's complex view of the world and human life leads him to evade common philosophical perspectives and pitfalls in favor of his own more thorough, more psychological approaches. In this case he replaces the old metaphors of freedom and unfreedom, no longer useful to him, with his more favored metaphors of strength and weakness.

The relationship between the concept of instinct and its antithesis, cleverness, is also important to Nietzsche's thought. Nietzsche often presents the commonly considered virtue of cleverness as a vice, such as when he says of men that "They are clever, their virtues have clever fingers. But they lack fists, their fingers do not know how to hide behind fists," and "Many I found who were clever:they veiled their faces and muddied their waters that nobody might see through them, deep down."[108] Passages such as these point to Nietzsche's negative valuing of clever thinking. Clever fingers do not make fists; that is, clever thinking does not strive toward overcoming, but is rather caught up in the lower-order priorities of herd living. Clever thinking muddies waters; that is, cleverness aids deception rather than the search for truth at any cost, which is aided rather by faith in instinct. Nietzsche devalues cleverness because he believes that someone needs to be clever only if he is a dissimulator, trying to deceive both himself and others. In opposition to the vice of cleverness Nietzsche posits instinct as virtue, the faculty prompting the noble person to action. In *Beyond Good and Evil* he writes that "'Instinct' is of all the kinds of intelligence that have been discovered so far—the most intelligent."[109] The greater value given to instinct over and against mere cleverness or reason begins with Zarathustra, and is continued and elaborated upon throughout the later works.

---

[108] *Zarathustra*, 282 and 286.
[109] *BGE*, 337.

As late as *Twilight of the Idols* Nietzsche writes that "Honest things, like honest men, do not carry their reasons in their hands like that."[110] Cleverness and reason are associated with thinking too much about matters which ought to be done, not thought. They are associated with justifying an inherited way of life whereas instinct is associated with creativity and the creation of new values, concepts of great importance to Nietzschean ethics. It is faith in instinct that goes along with having overcome resentment, having come to terms with fate and the eternal recurrence. If one is still resorting to cleverness to get by in life, one is a long way from self-overcoming. In fact, says Nietzsche, "To *have* to fight the instincts—that is the formula of decadence:as long as life is *ascending*, happiness equals instinct."[111] The struggle against instinct, often necessitated by thinking which gives primacy to reason, is anathema to the Nietzschean philosophies of self-overcoming, love of fate through willing the eternal recurrence, love of the overman, and everything elaborated here connected with these metaphors of ethical imperatives. If an individual striving toward what Nietzsche is describing here is behaving otherwise than his instincts advise him, he is somehow dissembling; or, in Nietzsche's words, he is decadent, or decaying. If, on the other hand, he is striving to overcome himself, which is to say his life is ascending, then his happiness derives from his living according to his instincts. So that Nietzsche's primacy of instinct is a crucial facet of his life philosophies.

Though much is implicit here with regard to the similar ethical positions of Nietzsche and Socrates, it is important to demonstrate how their thinking converges without being distracted by the different language they use in formulating their ethical worldviews and the different, often contradictory and mutually exclusive metaphysics from which these ethics derive. The immediately preceding discussion of Nietzsche's primacy of the instincts lends itself to a comparison with Socrates' position that right

---

[110] *TI*, 476.
[111] ibid., 479.

reason requires madness to approach the divine more closely. The texts lend themselves to a reading in which Socratic reason is more akin to Nietzschean instinct than Nietzschean reason, and therefore the Socratic imperative to reason agrees with the Nietzschean imperative to faith in instinct. The previous chapter argues that although Socrates is often characterized as asserting the primary importance of the human faculty of reason for the best possible earthly life and for the greatest ease of the ascension of the soul after death, in fact this is only true insofar as reason is understood much more broadly than is common. Reason in fact must include an element of what it is often though by definition to exclude, which is that which is irrational:often called emotion, passion, or divine inspiration, or madness. It is this divinely inspired madness, so critical to the best possible functioning of human reason for the Socrates of the *Phaedrus, Philebus, Symposium*, and elsewhere which is akin to Nietzsche's emphasis on instinct over what he calls reason, which is synonymous with cleverness or deceptive thinking and speaking, or rhetoric. Notice the similarities between the Nietzsche elaborated above, and the Socrates of the conclusion of the *Philebus*, after he has made his ironic attack on Lysias and is philosophizing so earnestly, and so compellingly. For Socrates, as he acknowledges quite explicitly in the *Phaedo*, the practice of philosophy is a preparation for death. For Nietzsche, as he begins to realize through Zarathustra and as he continues to believe even through and including the last, autobiographical *Ecce Homo*, it is the body that is primary. Either way, philosophy determines imperatives for the best possible earthly life, giving meaning to that very earthly life even if there is no anticipation of anything higher or later. Despite their clearly contradictory metaphysics, their ethics, here and throughout, are comfortably compatible.

This chapter demonstrates how the differences between Nietzsche and Socrates, once so significant, are no longer as important to current philosophy as their similarities. Nietzsche made much of his divergence from Plato, and often launched into vicious *ad hominem* attacks against both Plato and Socrates. Yet a closer examination of their work indicates that their differences are metaphysical, and perhaps Nietzsche's greatest evasion of metaphysics is not the evasion which appears in his writings, but the evasion taken hold in philosophy on account of his influence. Nietzsche held onto metaphysics at least enough to want to refute Platonic metaphysics, but now, only one hundred years later, what remains of importance is the ethical, which can be found in both Socrates and Nietzsche. Nietzsche may not have evaded metaphysics as much as he hoped in his own writings, but certainly his influence is responsible for the greater significance accorded ethics over metaphysics in current philosophizing. What follows is an analysis of literary texts, in which characters are analyzed from the perspectives of the Socratic and Nietzschean ethical imperatives demonstrated in the first two chapters. It is believed this keeps within the spirit of both Socrates and Nietzsche's emphases on creativity and art, as well as helping to point out the wider significance and implications of their philosophic imperatives, beyond just their own works and the Western philosophical tradition.

Chpater Three

Literary Possibilities for a
Philosophy of Everyday Life

*When a man finds that it is his destiny to suffer,
he will have to accept his suffering as his task; his
single and unique task. He will have to acknowledge the fact that even in suffering he is unique
and alone in the universe. No one can relieve
him of his suffering or suffer in his place. His
unique opportunity lies in the way in which he
bears his burden.* [112]

The epigram opening this chapter is from the psychiatrist Viktor Frankl,
and originates in his personal life-experience of imprisonment in concen-
tration camps. The passage reveals Frankl's often acknowledged theoretical
indebtedness to Dostoevsky, Schopenhauer, and Nietzsche, but its power
as a practical recommendation comes from its source in one man's suffering in the world. In this passage Frankl describes the phenomenon of individual suffering, alluding to his theory that the individual is responsible
for creating meaning and value in his life. *Man's Search for Meaning*, his
personal account of his own experiences and how those experiences led to
the development of his philosophy, abounds in evidence for and examples
of this belief. Philosophically, Frankl's ideas are as compelling as those of
Socrates and Nietzsche. And like Socrates and Nietzsche, the fact that the

---

[112] Frankl, Viktor.*Man's Search for Meaning.*Ilse Lasch, trans.Simon and
Schuster:New York, 1970, p, 78.

way he lived his own life informed his life philosophy makes that philosophy all the more compelling. In what follows, three literary characters are considered insofar as they exemplify some possibilities allowed by the philosophies of everyday life of Socrates and Nietzsche as developed in the previous two chapters. In this way, the wider import of philosophies which originated as individual worldviews is considered. Furthermore, connecting the fictional lives of these characters with the life and thought of Frankl reveals the complex connection among philosophy, literature, and life.

Aspects of the Socratic and Nietzschean influences are manifest in the protagonists of representative literary works from three different European countries. Ivan Denisovich Shukhov, from Aleksandr Solzhenitsyn's *One Day in the Life of Ivan Denisovich*, exemplifies Nietzschean joyful affirmation and creativity despite formidable difficulties. Examining Ivan Denisovich helps bring out more clearly elements of Nietzsche's philosophy of everyday life considered above. Joseph K., the protagonist of Franz Kafka's *The Trial*, also presents an interesting example. In some superficial ways K. is similar to Shukhov, especially when compared to the third literary character considered here, Camus' Meursault. K. seems to make an earnest effort in the process of his life, and the criminal trial which has come to dominate it. Yet K. is somehow misguided, always struggling fruitlessly in inherently unproductive directions while ignoring the indications of his downfall all around him. In this respect K. illustrates one way of reacting to the loss of Platonism as a viable belief system in the modern world. For Socrates, a belief in Platonic ideals justified and imparted meaning to his own earthly endeavors. K. fails to realize that the outside meaning he is searching for to make sense of the strange turn of events in his life is no longer there. And contrary to the Nietzschean imperative, K. is unable to accept his fate, and rather than struggle to comport himself well within it, he struggles against it, without success.

Albert Camus' Meursault, from *The Stranger*, is much different from both Shukhov and K., in that he is totally indifferent to the exigencies of his everyday life, from the most quotidian to the most extreme. Whereas Shukhov attempts to recreate himself through his suffering in accordance with the Nietzschean imperative, an imperative which K. merely contradicts, Meursault removes himself as much as possible from the course of his own life. Meursault illustrates a different reaction than K. to the same predicament:the loss of Platonism as a viable metaphysics. The lack of outside meaning informing his own life which makes K. ineffective, leads Meursault to nihilism. Further, Meursault seems always to rely on a too narrowly construed Socratic notion of attaining truth through reason, introspection, and abnegation. In what follows, analyses of these novels within the context of the Socratic and Nietzschean imperatives will make these assertions more clear.

In order to make more clear the relationships between these three novels and Socrates and Nietzsche's philosophies, this chapter will examine the ways in which these characters conduct themselves in the present moment. The various ways in which they relate their present to past events and future hopes indicates the philosophy of everyday life at work in the character. It is instructive to see the importance of environmental factors, as they contribute to the quality of the character's present moment, and his behavior within it. It is also interesting to consider the ways in which the characters relate themselves to others, insofar as this further reveals their attitudes within the present moment. So that an examination of these three characters will yield examples of the possibilities suggested by the philosophies of everyday life previously elaborated. Of the three characters mentioned, it is Shukhov who is most clearly in the spirit of Nietzsche and Frankl. Joseph K. seems almost willfully self-destructive in comparison, and Meursault unable or unwilling to make any effort to affect his life. Joseph K. and Meursault struggle equally unsuccessfully and in different ways with the collapse of Platonism. Shukhov, on the contrary, demonstrates the possibility provided by the Nietzschean reversal of Platonism and the ethics that reversal suggests.

An overview of the circumstances surrounding each character provides an opportunity to examine the substance of the character's life philosophy.

Viktor Frankl often recalls a line of Nietzsche's, "He who has a *why* to live for can bear with almost any *how*," in order to indicate the greater importance of an individual's comportment within his circumstances over and above those circumstances themselves.[113] Frankl comes back to that line again and again in connection with his various observations and experience in the camps. Camus' Meursault comes to a similar realization, recalling a belief of his dead mother's, "that in the long run one gets used to anything."[114] He reformulates this view in his own words, observing, "I've often thought that had I been compelled to live in the trunk of a dead tree, with nothing to do but gaze up at the patch of sky just overhead, I'd have got used to it by degrees."[115] Meursault's realization that he can get used to anything comes to him, like Frankl's, while imprisoned, and is expounded upon further by a number of interesting passages. As he grows accustomed to his imprisonment, he slowly stops thinking like a free man. He says of himself at that time that, "I had prisoner's thoughts," and gives as an example:

> Sometimes I would exercise my memory on my bedroom and, starting from a corner, make the round, noting every object I saw on the way. At first it was over in a minute or two. But each time I repeated the experience, it took a little longer. I made a point of visualizing every piece of furniture, and each article upon or in it, and then every detail.... With the result that after a few weeks, I could spend hours merely in listing the objects in my bedroom.[116]

---

[113] ibid., 76.

[114] Camus, Albert. *The Stranger.* Stuart Gilbert, trans. Vintage Books: New York, 1946, p. 96.

[115] *Stranger.*, 95.

[116] ibid., 95, 98.

Meursault is able to tolerate the loneliness and boredom of this phase of his existence by a conscious effort toward changing his thinking. Rather than torture himself by thinking like a free man, knowing he is not and most likely will never again be free, he accommodates his thinking to his unfreedom. In this way, he creates his own kind of freedom. This is very similar to some ill-received advice of Alyoshka the Baptist to Shukhov:"What good is freedom to you? If you're free, your faith will soon be choked by thorns! Be glad you're in prison. Here you have time to think about your soul."[117] Neither Meursault nor Shukhov is religious. Meursault resigns himself to his circumstances in a way similar to Alyoshka's suggestion on account of necessity, irrespective of faith. Shukhov uses his time in prison for introspection which, like for Frankl, allows him to create meaning and value in his life. This is perhaps similar to the advice "think about your soul," if "soul" is construed broadly, as suggested in connection with Nietzsche in the previous chapter.

Meursault cannot help but notice the human ability to get used to anything, yet he seems not to wish to get anywhere with this observation. Shukhov takes note of that same phenomenon, but unlike Meursault he goes somewhere in his thinking with that knowledge. This is evident in the small pleasures Shukhov takes in his life whenever he can, and also in the profound realizations he comes to during his daily routine of camp life and his ongoing introspection. Shukhov is happy when his day's gruel is substantial, which is the case on the day in which the novel's action takes place. And Shukhov is aware of the significance of his happiness. The reader learns that "The great news was that the gruel was good today, the very best, oatmeal gruel."[118] And to further illustrate the significance of the ability to take pleasure in this fact, the reader learns how "Shukhov had fed any amount of oats to horses as a youngster and never thought

---

[117] Solzhenitsyn, Aleksandr.*One Day in the Life of Ivan Denisovich.*H. T. Willetts, trans.Farrar, Straus, Giroux:New York, 1991, p. 177.

[118] ibid., 76.

that one day he'd be breaking his heart for a handful of the stuff."[119] Shukhov's happiness is not dependent only upon gruel; earning an extra portion of bread or a bit of food from another prisoner's parcel is equally pleasing to him. Perhaps it is understandable that a prisoner could take pleasure in his food, but Shukhov is not merely perpetuating his existence, he is imparting meaning to it. It is not just food that pleases him, but accomplishing a great deal of work with his gang at the day's site. Near the end of the workday he is pleased by what he has accomplished, and only stops working at the absolute last moment: "Shukhov looked over his shoulder. Yes, the sun was going down. A reddish sun in a sort of grayish mist. We're really getting somewhere now. Couldn't be better."[120] It is Shukhov's comportment within the severity and absurdity of his situation which demonstrates that he is, to borrow a phrase Frankl often borrows from Dostoevsky, worthy of his suffering.[121] Both Meursault and Shukhov accept and come to terms with their fate more or less in accordance with Nietzsche's doctrine of *amor fati*. However whereas Meursault accepts it indifferently, Shukhov accepts it as a joyful challenge, and responds to it with creative valuing.

Unlike Shukhov, Meursault is never happy. The whole of *One Day in the Life of Ivan Denisovich* takes place in prison, but it is only in the second half of *The Stranger* that Meursault finds himself in a similar circumstance. Prior to his crime and imprisonment, however, Meursault's freedom is wasted on him. There are numerous instances of Meursault's indifference to his own life. One is his relationship with his girlfriend, Marie. He is not hostile or mean to her, which would require as much of an emotional investment as love. He is consistently and completely indifferent: "A

---

[119] ibid., 77.

[120] ibid., 108.

[121] "Dostoevski said once, 'there is only one thing that I dread:not to be worthy of my sufferings.'" *Man's Search*, 66. And, "If someone now asked of us the truth of Dostoevski's statement that flatly defines man as a being who can get used to anything, we would reply, 'Yes, a man can get used to anything, but do not ask us how'" ibid., 16.

moment later she asked me if I loved her. I said that sort of question had no meaning, really; but I supposed I didn't."[122] Meursault is so removed from his own emotional life that the question of his love for Maria is a nonissue. If he has to commit himself to a response, he assumes the answer is no. Meursault gives himself many opportunities to reiterate this opinion:

> Marie came that evening and asked me if I'd marry her. I said I didn't mind; if she was keen on it, we'd get married.
> Then she asked me again if I loved her. I replied, much as before, that her question meant nothing or next to nothing—but I supposed I didn't.
> "If that's how you feel," she said, "why marry me?"
> I explained that it had no importance really, but, if it would give her pleasure, we could get married right away. I pointed out that, anyhow, the suggestion came from her; as for me, I'd merely said, "Yes."
> Then she remarked that marriage was a serious matter.
> To which I answered: "No."[123]

The passage continues in the same vein. Meursault remains unmoved by his girlfriend's love for him, but also by the very ideas of love and marriage. Love means nothing, marriage is not serious. Socrates attaches a great importance to love, believing it a necessary component of human reason. Meursault is indifferent, but not reasonable in the redefined Socratic sense.

Meursault maintains a similar aloofness in all of his other relationships. It is not only love and marriage that fail to effect him, but also friendship, enmity, violence, and, as the novel concludes, his own liberty. It is Meursault's friendship with Raymond Sintès that leads to the crime which concludes the first part of the novel. Despite the clearly significant impact

---

[122] *Stranger*, 44.
[123] ibid., 52–53.

of his relationship with Raymond on his life, Meursault is as detached from it as he is from his relationship with Marie. Early in their friendship, Raymond asks Meursault, "'So now we're pals, ain't we?' I kept silence and he said it again. I didn't care one way or the other, but as he seemed so set on it, I nodded and said, 'Yes.'"[124] The extent of Meursault's aloofness is such that it is not simply that Raymond values their friendship more, but that Meursault does not care any more about the impact of their friendship on his own life than he does about his friend. In other words, he seems not to care about himself any more than about Raymond.

This indifference toward himself as well as toward others is also evident in his relationship with his employer. Just prior to his exchange with Marie quoted above, Meursault's employer approaches him with the possibility of relocating to Paris, receiving this unanticipated response: "I told him I was quite prepared to go; but really I didn't care much one way or the other," and Meursault continues, quite presciently considering his later imprisonment, "One never changed his way of life; one life was as good as another, and my present one suited me quite well."[125] Meursault cannot envision a life that is better than his current one in virtue of taking place in a different location, so his employer's question of relocation has as little meaning for him as his girlfriend's questions of love and marriage. The extent to which Meursault holds this opinion is demonstrated by his reaffirmation of it in many different ways when imprisoned later in the novel, as demonstrated below.

Meursault's only reaction to the typically bizarre exchange with his employer is the acknowledgment that, "I'd have preferred not to vex him."[126] It is nothing to Meursault to remain where he is or move to Paris, if anything his concern is not to bother his employer unnecessarily. Matters of immediate concern to his life consistently fail to move him: his relationship with his girlfriend; his friendships; his employment; even

---

[124] ibid., 41.

[125] ibid., 52.

[126] ibid.

where he will live. The same indifference comes to play in the second part of the novel in connection with Meursault's crime, arrest, imprisonment, trial, and sentence. Reflecting on an early interaction with his lawyer, during which Meursault displayed his customary indifference to his mother's death, among other things, he puts his feelings in this telling way:

> Soon after this he left, looking quite vexed. I wished he had stayed longer and I could have explained that I desired his sympathy, not for him to make a better job of my defense, but, if I might put it so, spontaneously. I could see that I got on his nerves; he couldn't make me out, and, naturally enough, this irritated him. Once or twice I had a mind to assure him that I was just like everybody else; quite an ordinary person. But really that would have served no great purpose, and I let it go—out of laziness as much as anything else.[127]

Just like with his employer, Meursault's concern is having "vexed" his lawyer. Meursault's desire not to irritate people is taken to an absurd extreme, just as Socrates' opposite desire to provoke people can seem extreme. Meursault's desire to explain himself to his lawyer is not to improve his defense, much unlike Joseph K.'s interactions with his lawyer, rather simply to reassure him. And like so much else in his life, Meursault's reason for not explaining himself is his laziness, a symptom of his indifference. This indifference become even more startling when compared to matters which do concern him, such as the dampness of the roller towel in his office restroom, or the clothes his friend wears on their outing to the beach.[128] Meursault is resigned to the loss of Platonic

---

[127] ibid., 81.

[128] "Before leaving for lunch I washed my hands.I always enjoyed doing this at midday.In the evening it was less pleasant, as the roller towel, after being used by so many people, was sopping wet.I once brought this to my employer's notice.It was regrettable, he agreed—but to his mind a mere detail" ibid., 30.And, "Presently we heard Raymond shutting his door.He was wearing blue trousers, a short-sleeved white shirt, and a straw hat.I noticed that his forearms were rather hairy, but the skin was very white beneath.The straw hat made Marie giggle.Personally, I was rather put off by his getup" ibid., 60.

eternal and unchanging truths as a source of meaning for human life, and is unable to create a life for himself without those truths.

Shukhov's optimism despite his pessimistic situation contrasts with Meursault's ongoing nonchalance. Joseph K.'s conduct contrasts with Meursault's also, but his character demonstrates an entirely different, less reassuring ethical possibility from that demonstrated by Shukhov. Whereas Shukhov maintains his struggle for a meaningful existence and Meursault exhibits resignation to whatever will be his lot, Joseph K. seems impotent to control even his own reactions to his circumstances in the way Shukhov does, and to lack the awareness of his impotence with respect to fate that Meursault demonstrates. Whereas Meursault is resigned to the loss of Platonism, K. is still struggling against that loss without ever coming to terms with it.

From the very beginning of *The Trial* there is the indication that Joseph K. will not be able to make himself understood by his captors, or to behave in a way that will improve his situation. The reader learns of this early realization of K.'s:"Although he realized at once that he shouldn't have spoken aloud, and that by doing so he had, in a sense, acknowledged the stranger's right to oversee his actions, that didn't seem important at the moment."[129] Even at the earliest point of his ordeal, there is a sense of impotence and inevitability associated with Joseph K.'s situation. K. thinks he has altered his circumstances by choosing to speak rather than keep silent. He fears that he may somehow have legitimated the absurdity of his situation. Yet, in truth it makes no difference here or anywhere whether K. speaks or not, or what he says. This is so because the outside truths K. assumes, no longer exist.

Shortly after the realization just quoted, an inspector has this advice for K.:"Think less about us and what's going to happen to you, and instead

---

[129] Kafka, Franz. *The Trial.* Breon Mitchell, trans. Schocken Books:New York, 1998, p. 4.

think more about yourself. And don't make such a fuss about how innocent you feel; it disturbs the otherwise not unfavorable impression you make. And you should talk less in general.... "[130] This advice seems more like a general recommendation for conduct in daily life than a specific commentary on K.'s reaction to the proceedings against him. K. is convinced of his own innocence, but his conviction is based on appeals to outside justifications which are no longer valid.

Joseph K. is unable to make himself understood, and Meursault has no wish to speak a word of explanation. During each of the critical events of *The Stranger*, Meursault realizes the uselessness of speech. He does not believe he will be able to make himself clear to his interlocutors, and he does not feel any desire even to make the effort. This is true of his arrest and trial. Meursault explains himself to the examining magistrate in this way, "Well, I rarely have anything much to say. So, naturally I keep my mouth shut."[131] During the trial itself Meursault recalls to himself a similar sentiment, in response to an urge he experiences to try to explain himself, "However, on second thoughts, I found I had nothing to say."[132] In his interactions with his examining magistrate, during the course of his trial, and even when evading the prison chaplain while awaiting his execution, Meursault maintains his unwillingness or inability to plead his case. He says of his lack of desire to see the chaplain that, "I have nothing to say to him, don't feel like talking."[133] Perhaps if this desire not to speak had appeared suddenly as a result of the traumatic events at the beach, it would be more understandable. But this aspect of Meursault's character is consistent throughout the novel. As early as his mother's funeral, it is not so much that Meursault is at a loss for words, as he simply is entirely unmotivated to talk at all.

---

[130] ibid., 14.
[131] *Stranger*, 82.
[132] ibid., 124.
[133] ibid., 135.

This taciturn character trait of Meursault's is one of the very first things the reader learns about him. On his way to the funeral he does not wish to speak to the soldier sitting next to him on the bus. "I wasn't in a mood for talking," Meursault explains.[134] He feels the same way about the employee at his mother's old age home, "I had nothing to say, and the silence lasted quite a while."[135] It is not surprising that this same silence characterizes his relationship with Maria, and his unwillingness to respond to her questions about love and marriage, "To which I had nothing to say, so I said nothing."[136] Meursault's lack of voice contrasts with the impotence of his voice on the rare but significant occasions during which he uses it. When the examining magistrate is railing against his lack of religion, Meursault evades him in this way: "As I usually do when I want to get rid of someone whose conversation bores me, I pretended to agree."[137] Meursault cannot express himself, so he agrees with the examining magistrate. Similarly, Meursault is unable to persuade the prison chaplain of the certainty of his beliefs, but rather rails against him at great length and unsuccessfully. Meursault is certainly very out of character here, although he remains unable to make any sort of human connection with the chaplain. Meursault describes, "Then, I don't know how it was, but something seemed to break inside of me, and I started yelling at the top of my voice. I hurled insults at him, I told him not to waste his rotten prayers on me.... I poured out on him all the thoughts that had been simmering in my brain."[138] When Meursault finally has something to say, it serves so little purpose as to be tantamount to saying nothing at all. He is not able to satisfy his desire to explain himself to the prison chaplain, rather he merely elicits some unwanted and condescending pity.

---

[134] ibid., 2.
[135] ibid., 12.
[136] ibid., 53.
[137] ibid., 86.
[138] ibid., 151.

Another example of Meursault's conversational successes is even more telling. During his second altercation with the Arabs on the beach, Meursault talks Raymond into handing over the revolver. "I thought quickly," Meursault says, and then, "'Listen,' I said to Raymond. 'You take on the fellow on the right and give me your revolver. If the other one starts making trouble or gets out his knife, I'll shoot.'"[139] Here Meursault is at his most thoughtful and persuasive. Trying to prevent an inevitable tragedy and protect his friend, he cleverly takes possession of the revolver. Unfortunately, when he returns to that same spot alone, it is he who shoots the Arab. Meursault is successful in preventing Raymond, whose friendship he does not value at all, from shooting his enemy. Subsequently, it is Meursault rather than Raymond who shoots and kills the Arab with whom he has no quarrel, goes to jail and on trial, and is sentenced by a jury to death at a public execution. In general, Meursault is unable to explain himself and he knows it, and does not try. When he does make the effort, it is without the success for which he may have hoped.

Meursualt lives without much need for conversation. Socrates lives as though conversation were among the greatest goods available to human kind. Socrates relies on conversation as a means for bringing the imperfection of his knowledge closer to divine and eternal truths. For Meursault, in the absence of any eternal and unchanging truths there is no need to try to pursue those truths. So Meursault is rarely motivated to pursue a conversation. Unlike Meursault, Joseph K. struggles always in the wrong directions, including in his doomed speeches and conversations. He is filled with false confidences about his innocence and his persuasiveness, and immune to having his attention drawn to the futility of his actions. In fact, others offer K. the same manner of multipurpose advice as the initial inspector's to "talk less in general." After his powerful self-defense at his first hearing, which is reminiscent of Socrates' speeches of the *Apology*, his examining magistrate has this reproval of his conduct:"'I just wanted to

---

139 ibid., 71, 72.

draw your attention to the fact,' said the examining magistrate, 'that you have today deprived yourself—although you can't yet have realized it—of the advantage that an interrogation offers to the arrested man in each case.'"[140] At this point it is clear even to K. that the examining magistrate is not being entirely truthful. K. is more without advantages than he knows, but he has not suddenly deprived himself of them. It is his on-going unawareness of his inability either to provide or limit his advantages that is responsible for the limitations on his existential possibilities. He realizes the truthlessness of the examining magistrates reproval, however he does not make the greater realization that he is as powerless to procure advantages as to deprive himself of them.

It is possible that K., like Meursault, achieves some sort of resignation as he approaches death, but early in the novel he pursues in the futility of his optimism. For example, when looking for the room in which the preceding quote takes place, K. becomes upset that the court has not provided him with more accurate directions, making this resolution:"He was annoyed that they hadn't described the location of the room more precisely; he was certainly being treated with strange carelessness or indifference, a point he intended to make loudly and clearly."[141] The contrast between this resolution and the examining magistrates reproach indicates the doomed uselessness of K.'s efforts, and the strange fact of his inability to recognize that uselessness. It is a matter of no consequence whether or not K. is treated differently, because K. will not be able to succeed regardless of circumstances. The inevitability of K.'s bad end results from K. himself, and the way he lives his life, not the circumstances of that life as imposed on him from without by others. Without realizing this, nothing else will help Joseph K.

One recurring rhetorical device of *The Trial* that supports this reading of K.'s behavior is the inability to decide between rival courses of action.

---

[140] *Trial*, 52–53.
[141] ibid., 39.

The first instance of this in the text seems to be insignificant. K's uncle has arrived from the country, and suggests that K. spend some time there, citing some speciously convincing reasons. K. avers, "Except I don't think a stay in the country would be to my advantage, even in the sense you intend, because it would imply flight and a guilty conscience. And although they can certainly follow me more closely here, I can also take a more active role in the case."[142] Here K.'s uncle agrees, confessing, "I only made that suggestion because I was afraid if you remained here your case would be damaged by your own indifference, and I thought it better to act in your behalf. But if you intend to pursue it as strongly as possible yourself, that's obviously far better."[143] If K. is going to behave one way, perhaps he should travel to the country. If another, he should remain in the city. However, remaining in the city will not help K. any more than traveling to the country will harm him. No external circumstance will affect his ability to succeed in his trial. This early instance of this type of indecision indicates the impossibility of determining the superiority of one course of events over another. A case can be made for going to the country, and another, equal case can be made for remaining in the city. Which is preferable depends upon K.'s ability to parlay the choice into success with his trial. Unfortunately, K. will be unable to make use of either eventuality, and it is clear to the reader that had he gone to the country, his efforts would have been equally fruitless.

Another, later instance of this device is K.'s discussion with the manufacturer about whether or not he should visit the painter Titorelli. The manufacturer advises K., "But you shouldn't neglect even the smallest item in these matters," and proceeds to suggest that he visit Titorelli, a painter whose main source of income is in painting portraits of the court's judges.[144] Yet even as he is advising K. in this way, the manufacturer

---

[142] ibid., 95.
[143] ibid.
[144] ibid., 135.

acknowledges, "Of course Titorelli gossips a lot, and I often have to turn him off, not simply because he surely lies as well.... "[145] K. should not neglect even the smallest matter; after all, sometimes seemingly small matters have large and important consequences. Therefore, K. should visit Titorelli. Of course, Titorelli lies and gossips; therefore, K. should not consult Titorelli. Once again, there is the impossibility of choosing between rival courses of action. This reading is further supported by the manufacturer's ultimate recommendation to K., which seems to intimate the reading argued for here. The manufacturer concludes his advice in this unhelpful fashion, basically saying nothing at all:

> Of course—let me add this—you mustn't feel obliged to actually visit Titorelli just because I'm the one who advised you to do so. No, if you think you can get along without him, it would be better to leave him out of it entirely. Perhaps you already have some precise plan Titorelli might disturb. Then no, you most assuredly shouldn't go. A person is naturally reluctant to allow himself to be advised by a fellow like that. As you wish, then.[146]

The manufacturer presents K. with two options:visit Titorelli; or, do not visit Titorelli. Explaining the benefits of each possibility, it becomes clear that there is no way to decide between them. Furthermore, on this reading of K.'s futility, each choice is equally indifferent. Just as K.'s uncle and K. wavered in their decision regarding going to the country or remaining in the city, the manufacturer wavers in his recommendation that K. visit with Titorelli. And just as the uncle and K.'s indecisiveness indicates, when read as argued here, the indifference which either choice will make on the progress and outcome of K.'s trial, so will K.'s choice to visit Titorelli ultimately serve no useful purpose.

K.'s interaction with Titorelli reveals another aspect of the ultimate unimportance of the decisions available to K. This is revealed to the reader

---

[145] ibid., 136.
[146] ibid., 137.

in at least two ways:the absurdity of Titorelli's overvaluing K.'s assertion of innocence; and the seriousness with which K. ultimately takes Titorelli's information. Titorelli is the first person ever to ask K. openly if he is innocent, to which K. authoritatively responds in the affirmative, "Suddenly he lifted his head again and said:'If you're innocent, then the matter is really quite simple.'K.'s face clouded over; this so-called confidant of the court was talking like an ignorant child."[147] There is a difficulty with K.'s assertion of innocence, regardless of whether or not it is true. In fact, the progress of the novel makes K.'s guilt or innocence a matter of secondary importance. The court seeks out the guilty. There is already an assumption of K.'s guilt. Further, as K. and Titorelli agree regarding public perception of the court, "'But they're all in agreement that charges are never made frivolously, and that the court, once it brings a charge, is convinced of the guilt of the accused, and that it is difficult to sway them from this conviction.''Difficult?' asked the painter, throwing one hand in the air. 'The court can never be swayed from it.'"[148] Already, early in their exchange, there is what for K. must be a devastating contradiction. If he is innocent, he has nothing to worry about. However, if he has been accused, then the court is convinced of his guilt and cannot be dissuaded. K. is trapped in a situation he is powerless to change, a situation strangely similar to those of Frankl and Shukhov. But his interaction with Titorelli becomes even more frustrating.

Soon Titorelli reassures K. with the following incredible information, which somehow seems reasonable to K., even filling him with false hope. Regarding the impossibility of proving his innocence to the court, Titorelli demonstrates for K. that the court is

'Impervious only to proof brought before the court,' said the painter, and lifted his forefinger, as if K. had missed a subtle

---

147 ibid., 148.
148 ibid., 149.

distinction. 'But it's another matter when it come to behind-the-scenes efforts, in the conference rooms, in the corridors, or, for example, even here in the atelier.' What the painter now said seemed less improbable to K.; on the contrary it stood in close agreement with what K. had heard from others as well. Yes, it was even filled with hope.[149]

Here what is so hopeful to K. is an absurdity even greater than that of the question of his innocence or guilt before the court. K. cannot make a case for himself to the court, however the painter, having just met K., can persuade the judges of his innocence informally. Titorelli soon compounds the absurdities and contradictions by explaining the various options available to K., none of which is, or even should be, hopeful to him. Titorelli seems at least implicitly to acknowledge the absurdity of what he has just told K. when he advises him, upon his departing, in a manner reminiscent of the manufacturers advice to K. about Titorelli himself: "You probably still haven't reached a decision with regard to my suggestions. I approve of that. In fact I would have advised against a quick decision. There's only a hair's difference between the advantages and disadvantages. Everything has to be weighed quite carefully. Of course you don't want to lose too much time either."[150] Once again there is the implication that no matter how long K. deliberates it is too long, because the "hair's difference" is in fact no difference at all in terms of affecting the outcome of the trial.

Meursault disagrees with Socrates as to the usefulness of conversation because of contradictory metaphysical assumptions. Meursault believes himself to derive no benefit from conversation, whereas Socrates derives the greatest benefit. Similarly, Joseph K. has no means available to him for assessing the benefits of choosing between different courses of action. In the absence of outside truths against which to measure his own options,

---

[149] ibid., 150–151.
[150] ibid., 162.

K., despite his former success as a banker, is unable to determine costs and benefits in order to arrive at decisions. Much to the contrary, Socrates appeals to the eternal and unchanging in determining the best possible course of his life. Real belief in Platonic metaphysics allows Socrates to justify his life in a way no longer available either to Meursault, in terms of his conversations, or to Joseph K., in terms of his decision-making.

The preceding examples illustrate that the choices available to Joseph K. are not real choices, in the sense both that they offer him no real options and that the fact of his choosing will make no difference to him in the last analysis. They are one example of his impotence with respect to the course of his life during his trial. Another example is his inability to clear his mind, focus his thinking, and concentrate on anything at all, neither business nor his personal problems, as the novel progresses. In this way K. is effected by his environment just as powerfully as Meursault. After his trial has been ongoing for some months, K. spends a typical workday in this way:"Instead of working he swung about in his chair, moved a few items around slowly on his desk, and then, without being aware of it, left his arm outstretched on the desktop and remained sitting motionless with bowed head."[151] On this particular day, K. is unable to concentrate on his work, instead thinking in circles about his trial. Later he is unable to concentrate on his business deal with the manufacturer, who then puts him in touch with Titorelli. His once productive time is now spent in this way:"He went to the window, sat down on the broad sill, held on tightly to the handle with one hand, and looked out onto the square.... He sat like that for a long time."[152] But it is not just that he is no longer able to concentrate on his work; that he is overwhelmed by circumstances he used to enjoy. He is also powerfully effected by environmental factors such as the bad air in the law offices, which cause K. the

---

[151] ibid., 111.
[152] ibid., 131.

same type of confusion as he experienced in his office in the passages just quoted.

The week after his initial inquiry, a court usher gives K. a tour of some of the law offices, during which K. first notices the bad effects of the air in the places he visits in connection with the trial. An employee of the offices draws K.'s attention to this fact, "The sun beats down on the attic beams and the hot wood makes the air terribly thick and stifling.... But as far as the air is concerned, on days when the traffic of involved parties is heavy you can hardly breathe, and that's almost daily.... But in the end people get quite used to the air."[153] In fact the employees get so used to it, that fresh air is offensive to them, as K. notices after the employee just quoted and another have helped him to the exit, "...he noticed they were unable to bear the comparatively fresh air from the stairway, accustomed as they were to the air in the offices of the court. They could hardly reply, and the young woman might have fallen had K. not shut the door as quickly as possible."[154] The phenomenon of bad air recurs whenever K. is in spaces associated with the court. When he is visiting Titorelli, whose apartment is in an attic and adjacent to law offices ("There are law offices in practically every attic"), he experiences a similar spell.[155] K. explains how"...the closeness in the room was inexplicable...it was the muggy atmosphere that rendered breathing difficult...this unpleasantness was intensified...."[156] Physical and psychological factors are closely related. The difficulties K. encounters in trying to take control of his trial are accompanied by physical ailments whenever he is in those situations having to do with the trial.

The connection between environmental factors and psychological state is even more pronounced for Meursault. Throughout the entire text of *The Stranger* Meursault's thinking is impaired at the most crucial times by

---

[153] ibid., 73–74.
[154] ibid., 79.
[155] ibid., 164.
[156] ibid., 148.

what for him appear to be extreme environmental conditions. The first instance of this is his mother's funeral at the outset of the novel, and many more instances follow. But the most significant is on the beach during the altercations with the Arabs. Meursault has three interactions with the Arabs. In the first he is with Raymond and Masson, and one of the Arabs cuts Raymond with a knife. Meursault is "feeling slightly muzzy," and tells the reader, "I wasn't thinking of anything, as all that sunlight beating down on my bare head made me feel half asleep."[157] As the Arabs approach, Meursault observes, "The sand was as hot as fire, and I could have sworn it was glowing red."[158] These impressions are more extreme variations of those he had during his mother's funeral procession. They create a sense of inevitability about the actions that are to come, especially in connection with Meursault's characteristic indifference. Soon after, Meursault and Raymond return to the same place, though it is unclear with what intentions. Meursault recalls:"It was like a furnace outside, with the sunlight splintering into flakes of fire on the sand and sea."[159] They see the two Arabs and Raymond hands Meursault his revolver, but nothing happens. They return to Masson's bungalow.

For whatever vague reasons, at this time Meursault walks back down the beach again rather than entering the bungalow. He describes the effects he observes the environment having on him in many similar passages, "As I slowly walked toward the boulders at the end of the beach I could feel my temples swelling under the impact of the light. It pressed itself on me, trying to check my progress. I gritted my teeth, I clenched my fists in my trouser pockets and keyed up every nerve to fend off the sun and the dark befuddlement it was pouring into me."[160] Meursault's normally clear-headed indifference is now compounded by the hot, bright

---

[157] *Stranger*, 66, 67.
[158] ibid., 68.
[159] ibid., 70.
[160] ibid., 73.

environment's impeding of his thinking. It is in this condition that he meets one of the Arabs for the third time since arriving at the beach. During the long standoff preceding the shooting, Meursault explains, "The heat was beginning to scorch my cheeks; beads of sweat were gathering in my eyebrows. It was just the same sort of heat as at my mother's funeral, and I had the same disagreeable sensations—especially in my forehead, where all the veins seemed to be bursting through the skin."[161] Just as at the funeral his indifference was compounded by an inability to ignore uncomfortable environmental influences, at the beach Meursault is practically incapacitated due to similar but more extreme circumstances.

Just prior to the shooting, Meursault describes how, "Beneath a veil of brine and tears my eyes were blinded; I was conscious only of the cymbals of the sun clashing on my skull…a fiery gust came from the sea, while the sky cracked in two, from end to end, and a great sheet of flame poured down through the rift."[162] He cannot see, blinded by sweat and tears from the sun; he cannot think on account of the severe heat. His customary indifference is now compounded by environmental factors. Meursault shoots the Arab in much the same way he vexes his employer and lawyer, and with much the same reaction. There is a certain inevitability associated with the shooting, and although Meursault does acknowledge that he has just experienced a life-changing event, nevertheless he seems typically unmoved by it.

Shukhov's dependence upon environmental factors is just as real as Meursault's, but the effect they have on him and his reactions to them are much different. Unlike the blinding sun and scorching heat Meursault describes, Shukhov describes conditions of incessant bitter cold. Shukhov says that the public thermometer hangs, "in a sheltered spot so that it would not fall too low…if it showed forty-one below, they weren't supposed to be marched out to work. But it was nowhere near forty today."[163]

---

[161] ibid., 75.

[162] ibid., 75, 76.

[163] *One Day*, 10.

In numerous places Shukhov describes the cold weather, its impact on daily life, and the ways the prisoners react to it. His descriptions are as numerous and consistent as Meursault's of the sun and heat. From his experience of the cold, Shukhov formulates this simple question pointing up the importance of empathy:"Can a man who's warm understand one who's freezing?"[164] Shukhov's experience of the cold is connected to his life-affirming worldview in the same way that Meursault's experience with his environment is connected to his indifference.

Nietzsche is aware of the importance of environment to human life. His belief in according appropriate concern to matters of region and weather is connected to his primacy of the body and the earth. These metaphysical beliefs strongly influence his ethical recommendations. Socrates both detaches himself from and takes an interest in his environment. In keeping with his belief that sense perceptions merely deceive and that true knowledge only arrives through reason, Socrates often maintains a total unawareness of what is going on around him. There are numerous instances of this in the dialogues, for example the beginning of the *Symposium.* Socrates is so concerned with his own process of introspection that he loses awareness of where he is or what he is doing. This is a characteristic famously mocked by Aristophanes. Yet elsewhere he is much different, such as at the beginning of and throughout the *Phaedrus.* Here Socrates is acutely aware of being outside of the city gates, barefoot, by a stream, and in the company of his friend. Matters of environment are of real concern to both Socrates and Nietzsche. The various ways in which Shukhov, Meursault, and Joseph K. function within their environments reflect the degrees to which they either suffer from the abandonment of Platonic ways of thinking or rejoice in accepting a Nietzschean personal responsibility for their unique and individual lives.

Meursault's indifference is further demonstrated in the way he perceives others. He is surprisingly unmoved by the presence of an old man called

---

[164] ibid., 24.

Pérez, a friend of his mother's, at her funeral, despite this description of him as he struggles to maintain the pace of the funeral procession:"The old boy's face, for instance, when he caught up with us for the last time, just outside the village. His eyes were streaming with tears, of exhaustion or distress, or both together. But because of the wrinkles they couldn't flow down. They spread out, crisscrossed, and formed a smooth gloss on the old, worn face."[165]Meursault is not able to make any sort of connection with the old man. Even more striking, Meursault is not even able to empathize in his thinking about the old man. Unlike Meursault, Shukhov is able to perceive others with empathy.

Consider Shukhov's perception of an old man he is otherwise as little familiar with as Meursault is with his mother's friend:

> With hunched-over lags all round, he was as straight-backed as could be. He sat tall, as though he'd put something on the bench under him. That head hadn't needed a barber for ages; the life of luxury had caused all his hair to fall out. The old man's eyes didn't dart around to take in whatever was going on in the mess, but stared blindly at something over Shukhov's head. He was steadily eating his thin skilly, but instead of almost dipping his head in the bowl like the rest of them, he carried his battered wooden spoon up high. He had no teeth left, upper or lower, but his bony gums chewed his bread just as well without them. His face was worn thin, but it wasn't the weak face of a burnt-out invalid, it was like dark chiseled stone...he refused to knuckle under....[166]

And the passage continues in the same vein. It is easy to see why Shukhov finds inspiration in his perception of this old man, in stark contrast to Meursault's unfeeling perception of Pérez. There are certain specific

---

[165] ibid., 21–22.

[166] *One Day*, 154–155.A similar passage describes Shukhov's work gang companion, Buynovsky, earlier in the text (82).

observations of Shukhov's which must surely give him hope. Shukhov surely must hope that his own spoon, his most valuable possession, will serve him as well as this old man's did.[167] Shukhov must hope that even when he loses the rest of his hair and teeth, he will still be able to eat his skilly and bread with dignity.[168] Meursault is without hope, and his perceptions of others are tainted with his hopelessness. So that when he perceives an old man such as Pérez, it is without any comprehension of the depth of human suffering beneath his wrinkled, tear-moistened visage. Shukhov, exhibiting on the contrary a life-affirming worldview, sees in an old man all his own hopes for living well despite suffering.

The preceding discussion focuses on the characters as they are in the present moment. However, it is equally important to examine the ways they view their past experiences, and anticipate the future. Shukhov's optimism is not on account of hope for the future. He knows that, "They could twist the law any way they liked. When your ten years were up, they could say good, have another ten," yet his feeling is, "When you're flat on your face there's no time to wonder how you got in and when you'll get out."[169] Shukhov realizes that he needs to create a life for himself without thought for a future, which is a profound realization. Certainly Meursault has a difficult time with these same types of thoughts as he awaits his execution. Shukhov asks himself, "Only—would they ever let him go? Maybe they'd slap another ten on him, just for fun?"[170] He is aware of the real hopelessness of his future freedom. His concern is for the present; for the creation of a meaningful life despite his suffering. Toward the end of the

---

[167] "Shukhov drew his spoon from his boot. That spoon was precious, it had traveled all over the north with him. He'd cast it himself from aluminum wire in a sand mold and scratched on it: 'Ust-Izhma, 1944'" (ibid., 16).

[168] "Shukhov had been knocking around for forty years, he'd lost half his teeth and was going bald...." (ibid., 44).

[169] ibid., 69.

[170] ibid., 44.

novel, this sentiment is expressed strongly, "For the moment he had only one thought:We shall survive. We shall survive it all. God willing, we'll see the end of it!"[171] These feelings are a remarkable accomplishment of Shukhov's, demonstrating his struggle to become worthy of his suffering. Meursault's vaguely parallel struggle offers similarities, and striking differences.

Through the first half of *The Stranger* and the trial that is the bulk of the second half, Meursault never gives a thought to the future or the past. He merely passes his daily life with very little interest. It is after he is sentenced to death that he begins to have the same thoughts with which Shukhov wrestles throughout that novel, though without arriving at the same conclusions. Shukhov lives without thoughts of a future he knows he may not have; Meursault fabricates a future he knows he cannot possibly have in order to be able to live in the present moment. Shortly after the end of his trial, Meursault daydreams about "circumventing the machine," by which he means that "The problem of a loophole obsesses me; I am always wondering if there have been cases of condemned prisoners' escaping from the implacable machinery of justice at the last moment, breaking through the police cordon, vanishing in the nick of time before the guillotine falls."[172] Although he never gave a single thought to questions about the meaning of his existence when free, nevertheless when he knows he is about to die Meursault gives his mind over to these types of fruitless flights of fancy.

His way of reassuring himself, however, is consistent with his earlier indifference. Meursault tells himself that "It's common knowledge that life isn't worth living, anyhow," and continues:"And, on a wide view, I could see that it makes little difference whether one dies at the age of thirty or threescore and ten—since, in either case, other men and women will continue living, the world will go on as before."[173] This almost Platonic per-

---

171 ibid., 153.
172 *Stranger*, 136.
173 ibid., 142–143.

spective, in which the general concept of living men and women is accorded greater value than individuals, including himself, agrees more with his earlier outlook than his imaginings of somehow escaping his fate. And the thoughts which end the novel continue to support this reading. Meursault lays his "heart open to the benign indifference of the universe," and acknowledges how, "all that remained to hope was that on the day of my execution there should be a huge crowd of spectators and that they should greet me with howls of execration."[174] In the last analysis, even the proximity and certainty of his death does not spur Meursault from his characteristic apathy.

Socrates and Nietzsche are in agreement about the importance of dying well. Socrates does not fear his own execution anymore than Meursault fears his, though Meursault gives more purchase to the possibility of escape. Socrates wishes to spend his last hours in conversation with his friends; Meursault wishes to be publicly disgraced. As he is executed, Joseph K. expresses a similar sentiment: "It seemed as though the shame was to outlive him."[175] Socrates was concerned for living well without the thought of death; Joseph K. remains concerned for his reputation even at the end of his trial. He truly seems to have learned nothing of his life, despite wanting to show that he has: "Do I want to show now that even a yearlong trial could teach me nothing? Do I want to leave the parting impression that I'm slow-witted? Shall they say of me that at the beginning of my trial I wanted to end it, and now, at its end, I want to begin it again? I don't want them to say that."[176] What he shows is that he continues to misunderstand where the potential for effective action in his life lies, and to misdirect his efforts in inherently fruitless directions. Even at the approach of death, Meursault and Joseph K. fail to redeem their lives.

---

[174] ibid., 154.
[175] *Trial*, 231.
[176] ibid., 228.

This discussion has demonstrated how three literary characters, when taken together, represent three of an infinite continuum of possibilities for a philosophy of everyday life. This discussion is not meant to exclude other possibilities or examples. It rather shows how three much different possibilities can emerge from a consideration of literary texts in conjunction with the life philosophies of Socrates and Nietzsche. Meursault, unable to make a commitment to his own life and resigned to his own death, reverts to nihilism in the absence of Platonic certainty. Joseph K., struggling impotently to make others accountable for a life for which only he can ultimately take responsibility, is unaware of the loss of the Platonic certainty he assumes is still able to give his life meaning. And Ivan Denisovich Shukhov, maintaining joyful affirmation and creativity in the midst of interminable imprisonment and suffering, creates a meaningful life in the absence of certainty in the creative spirit of Nietzsche and Frankl. With the observations of Viktor Frankl which opened this chapter in mind, it is clear to see how each character lived up to the challenges of his suffering.

Conclusion

Relying on Platonic metaphysics, Socrates is able to derive ethical recommendations which are well supported and justified. Through conversation, Socrates is able to demonstrate to any interlocutor why intelligence is preferable to madness; reason to emotion; justice to injustice; philosophy to the pursuit of pleasure. Socrates can lead any interlocutor to the same observations he has made, because there is actually something out there his thinking and questioning is approaching. The additional, often overlooked aspect of Socratic thought is that his metaphysical dichotomies are not as far apart and independent of one another as they may seem.

What Socrates also demonstrates is that the practice of philosophy is not removed from everyday living, despite his being traditionally portrayed as believing this very thing. Reason is not detached from the irrational, nor is philosophy detached from pleasure. Socrates develops a complex ethical system with very real recommendations and imperatives for living the best possible life. But his recommendations are supported by their reliance on an eternal and unchanging metaphysical system, the truth of which is accessible to anyone who sets his mind to approaching it.

Nietzsche puts forth several strongly urged ethical imperatives. Yet unlike Socrates, he is thinking about ethics outside of a context of eternity and certainty. So unlike Socrates, Nietzsche cannot rest his ethics on any metaphysical foundation. Nietzsche must make his recommendations in the absence of God, truth, certainty, even a realm of perfect forms. Nietzsche's ethical system derives entirely from the simple fact of existing bodily on the earth, with no other justification than earthly, temporal, mortal existence. Through theories such as the eternal recurrence and recommendations such as *amor fati*, Nietzsche is able to develop an ethics without metaphysics.

Joseph K., Meursault, and Shukhov illustrate three different reactions to Socratic and Nietzschean worldviews. Joseph K. lives as if he believes he is still in Plato's world. Like Socrates, he assumes the existence of outside truths on which he can rely to support and defend him. It is his inability to come to terms with the absence of these truths and create a meaningful life for himself despite that absence that dooms him to futility in life and an undignified and misunderstood death.

Like K., Meursault is dependent on a Platonic way of thinking about life. Meursault differs from K. by realizing that the Platonic certainty K. still assumes is in fact to longer out there. Meursault reacts to this realization by feeling indifferent about his own life. His reaction is a kind of nihilism. For Meursault, in the absence of a Platonic type of metaphysics, nothing matters. Whereas K. does not realize the need to give value to his life, Meursault acts as though he believes he cannot give his life that value.

Unlike both Joseph K. and Meursault, Ivan Denisovich Shukhov is aware of the tenuousness of his existence, and able to make a life for himself in spite of that. Shukhov had as little means to contest his sentence and imprisonment as K., and is as aware of the hopelessness of his future as Meursault. However, he is able to act where K. is not, and able to create meaning where Meursault is not. In the absence of outside truths, Shukhov is nevertheless able to live an ethical life. Unlike K. and Meursault, Shukhov takes responsibility for creating a meaningful life and ethical existence for himself. In this way he has moved beyond Platonic constraint, in the direction of the individual responsibility of Nietzsche and Frankl.

The question remains, has Nietzsche adequately answered Socrates? That is, has he offered an ethics that does not require a metaphysics which is no longer a real option for belief. It is possible to read Socrates as suggesting an ethic which although based on Platonic metaphysics, does not require it. Socratic ethical imperatives retain their force even in the absence of Platonic ideals. Nietzsche struggles to give a meaning to the world which comes from the world itself rather than from beyond the world. But this may not be a sufficient response to the loss of Platonism. Or, Platonism may not be as unviable as so often assumed. After all, mathematics still relies on Platonic notions of outside and eternal truths, accessible in varying degrees to diligent seekers.

One difficulty with both Socratic and Nietzschean ethics is the lack of emphasis they give to the individual's functioning in society. Matters of concern to the individual are never connected to the community in which the individual lives. The significance of the individual's relating himself to others is only for the benefit of the individual himself. Clearly a satisfactory ethics cannot remain concerned only with the individual alone in the world. A new ethics must take into account many, many levels of individual involvement in larger and larger communities, even up to and including ecological matters.

The upshot of the ethical recommendations of this thesis for individuals might be called Platonic Nihilism. The loss of Plato's metaphysical beliefs does not require abandoning the ethics demonstrated by the life and philosophy of Socrates. Yet practicing that ethics in a meaningless world in order to create meaning for the world is a difficult task. The nausea of Zarathustra and the indifference of Meursault refuse to submit to Frankl's will to meaning or Nietzsche's joyful creation of value. There is always the sense that no matter how well Shukhov is able to live with his suffering, the suffering is still there. And this is true not just of extreme examples such as Shukhov and Frankl, but of everyone. The challenge is not merely to create an isolated but ethical life, but an ethical life within a world community. However, it is certainly instructive in thinking on these matters to consider the examples of Socrates and Nietzsche.

Bibliography

Camus, Albert. *The Stranger*. Stuart Gilbert, trans. Vintage Books:New York, 1946.

Frankl, Viktor. *Man's Search for Meaning*. Ilse Lasch, trans. Simon and Schuster:New York, 1970.

Jowett, B., trans. *The Dialogues of Plato*. Random House:New York, 1937, Vols. 1 and 2.

Kafka, Franz. *The Trial*. Breon Mitchell, trans. Schocken Books:New York, 1998.

Kaufmann, Walter, trans. *Basic Writings of Nietzsche*.Random House:New York, 1992

———. *The Portable Nietzsche*. Viking Penguin Inc.:New York, 1982.

Nietzsche, Friedrich. *Human All-Too-Human:A Book for Free Spirits*. R. J. Hollingdale, trans. Cambridge University Press:New York, 1994.

———. *Untimely Meditations*. R. J. Hollingdale, trans. Cambridge University Press:New York, 1995.

Rouse, W. H. D., trans. *Great Dialogues of Plato*. N. A. L.:New York, 1999.

Segal, Eric., ed. *The Dialogues of Plato*. Bantam:New York, 1986.

Solzhenitsyn, Aleksandr. *One Day in the Life of Ivan Denisovich*. H. T. Willetts, trans. Farrar, Straus, Giroux:New York, 1991.

www.ingramcontent.com/pod-product-compliance
Lightning Source LLC
Chambersburg PA
CBHW020248290526
45784CB00003B/1156